DINOSAUR
ENCYCLOPEDIA

igloo

This edition published in 2010
by Igloo Books Ltd
Cottage Farm,
Sywell,
NN6 0BJ
www.igloo-books.com

A copy of the British Library Cataloguing-in-Publication Data
is available from the British Library.

10 9 8 7 6 5 4 3 2 1
ISBN: 978 0 85734 189 1

Printed and manufactured in China

CONTENTS

MYA - Million years ago
BYA - Billion years ago

In the text, some words have been highlighted in **bold**. You will find more information about what these mean in the glossary.

5

DINOSAUR TIMELINE

Massive volcanic eruptions cause mass extinctions, wiping out 90% of marine life and 70% of land life!

First dinosaurs evolve. They are mostly fairly small (no more than 6 m (20 ft)), bipedal and fast moving. Marine reptiles like Icthyosaurs and Plesiosaurs also evolve at this time.

Dinosaurs dominant. First mammals evolve.

Mesozoic era

248 MYA – 65 MYA

Triassic period	Jurassic period
248 MYA – 206 MYA	206 MYA – 144 MYA

Stegosaurus

Eoraptor
Coelophysis

Sauropsids such as the archosaurs dominate. First cynodonts evolve.

Compsognathus
Diplodocus
Brachiosaurus

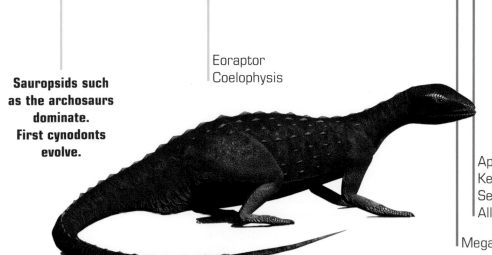

Apatosaurus
Kentrosaurus
Seismosaurus
Allosaurus

Megalosaurus

**Age of dinosaurs.
Dinosaurs are at
their peak in size,
variety and numbers
and dominate every
continent.**

**'K-T extinction'.
End of the
dinosaurs.**

Mesozoic era

248 MYA – 65 MYA

Cretaceous period

144 MYA – 65 MYA

Hadrosaurus
Velociraptor
Protoceratops

Centrosaurus
Troodon
Tyrannosaurus
Triceratops
Ankylosaurus
Edmontosaurus

Giganotosaurus
Spinosaurus

Argentinosaurus
Nodosaurus

Deinonychus

Acrocanthosaurus

Iguanadon

Baryonyx

FULL TIMELINE

Oceans and atmosphere form. Earliest life forms in oceans.

Trilobites dominate seas. Still no land life.

Earliest land plants appear.

Insects flourish. First reptiles evolve. Shrubs, ferns and trees dominate land.

Massive volcanic eruptions cause mass extinctions, wiping out 90% of marine life and 70% of land life!

Precambrian time 4.5–3.9 BYA			Palaeozoic era 540 MYA–248 MYA						
Hadean eon	Archean eon	Proterozoic eon	Cambrian period	Ordovician period	Silurian period	Devonian period	Carboniferous period	Permian period	

The Earth forms!

Sea plants begin photosynthesis.

First fish evolve.

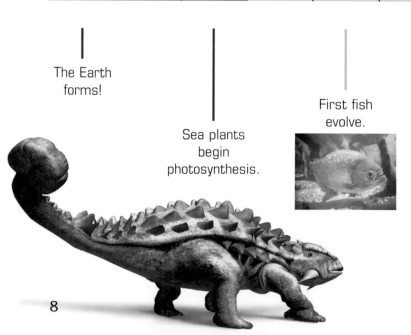

Fish dominate oceans. Spiders and mites are first land creatures. First amphibians evolve. First forests form.

Synapsids, such as Dimetrodon and amphibians such as Eryops dominate land.

Dinosaurs dominate. First mammals evolve.

'K-T extinction' (see page 206). End of the dinosaurs.

Mammals such as horses, bats and whales evolve.

Most modern birds and mammals have evolved.

'Great Ice Age' Neanderthals and Homo sapiens, or modern humans, evolve. Smilodon (sabre-toothed tiger), mastodons and mammoths evolve.

Mesozoic era 248 MYA–65 MYA			Cenozoic era 65 MYA–NOW							
			Tertiary period (65 MYA – 1.8MYA)						Quaternary period (1.8MYA – NOW)	
Triassic period	Jurassic period	Cretaceous period	Paleocene epoch	Eocene epoch	Oligocene epoch	Miocene epoch	Pliocene epoch		Pleistocene epoch	Holocene epoch

Sauropsids such as the archosaurs dominate. First cynodonts such as Cynognathus evolve. Marine reptiles evolve.

Age of dinosaurs. Dinosaurs are at their peak in size, variety and numbers and dominate every continent.

Mammals dominate. Early carnivores evolve.

Creodonts evolve. Modern mammals become dominant.

Hominids, the ape-like ancestors of humans evolve. Thylacosmilus and other early sabre-tooths evolve.

Last ice age ends. Human civilisation develops.

EVOLUTION

The Earth, and all life on it, is constantly changing. Life had been on Earth for at least 3,260 million years before the dinosaurs appeared. The Palaeozoic era was from 540 to 250 million years ago, and was known as 'the age of ancient life'.

By 245–235 million years ago (the **Mesozoic era**) a large number of reptiles roamed the earth. Some of these were dinosaurs, including herbivorous **rhynchosaurs** and carnivorous archosaurs.

Dinosaurs appeared about 230 million years ago, during the Triassic period (see page 22). Their **evolution** spread over the Jurassic and Cretaceaous periods (see pages 24–27), a total of 165 million years.

Dinosaurs completely dominated the land in a way that no other group of animals had done. Eight hundred species have been identified so far. No one knows where they came from.

Extinction

About 65 million years ago (the end of the Cretaceous period), 70 per cent of living species, including the dinosaurs and flying reptiles suddenly became extinct. Crocodiles and many other reptiles survived.

Tsunami breaking wave

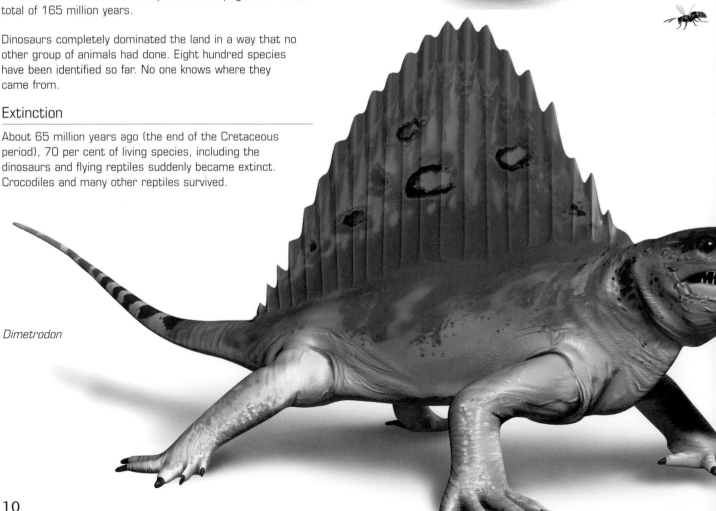

Dimetrodon

Archaeopteryx

Crocodile

The most popular explanation for this extinction is that an asteroid from space hit earth. There has been evidence of an enormous meteorite colliding with the Earth 65 million years ago. The meteorite may have been a single asteroid, bits from asteroid collisions, or debris from a comet. This would probably have thrown up an enormous amount of dust into the atmosphere which would have blocked out the sun and made the whole world dark for several months.

It might also have caused other natural disasters such as tsunamis and earthquakes. All plant life would have died, therefore plant eaters would not have been able to survive. In turn, carnivores would have had no food, causing them to die.

Other theories include a period of intense volcanic activity which may have caused changes such as global warming and effects on plant life. Another argument is that a drastic drop in sea level would have made the climate more extreme. It is difficult to imagine how this could have had such an effect. A third theory is that the climate changed enough to make earth too cold or hot for reptilian life, but this does not explain how some reptiles, such as crocodiles, survived.

The Cenozoic era began 65 million years ago and is often called the 'age of mammals', because mammals thrived at this time.

Scientists believe that birds are descendants of the dinosaurs. They may have come from small meat eaters such as Compsognathus (see page 62). You can see the similarity, especially when you compare the skeleton of dinosaurs to the skeleton of the oldest known bird, Archaeopteryx (see page 192), which lived about 140 million years ago.

11

ERYOPS

Primitive amphibian

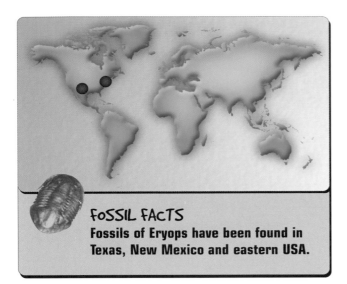

FOSSIL FACTS
Fossils of Eryops have been found in Texas, New Mexico and eastern USA.

Eryops was part of the Eryopidae family and probably lived during the Permian period (about 270 million years ago). This was a long time before the dinosaurs evolved. It was a primitive amphibian and looked a lot like the alligators that live today. The name Eryops means 'drawn-out face' because most of its skull was in front of its eyes.

Habitat

Because Eryops was an amphibian, this meant that it had to live near water (probably in swamps). This is so that it could lay its eggs. Amphibian eggs have no shells so they have to be laid in water or in a damp environment – otherwise they would dry out and die.

Appearance and diet

Although this meat eater had a short and stout body (it was about 1.5 m (5 ft) long), it was incredibly strong and was

probably one of the largest animals of its time. It had thick, strong bones, four short, but powerful legs and a short tail. Eryops also had a long and wide skull and lots of sharp teeth in its strong jaws.

Eryops' strong body was perfectly equipped for diving into the water and catching its prey. Its strength would also help to defend itself on land. Eryops probably ate mostly fish, small reptiles and other amphibians.

Predators

Eryops didn't have many predators, as they were one of the largest land animals, but they probably had to be wary of some of the Dimetrodon (see page 16), which moved faster than the Eryops on land.

In the water, the **Orthacanthus** may have preyed upon the Eryops, which would not have been able to move as quickly. However, some scientists believe the Eryops moved quicker in water than on land, where it may not even have been able to run.

MEGA FACTS

- Eryops had a primitive ear which allowed it to hear airborne sound.

- The fang-like teeth weren't actually used for chewing. Eryops would grasp its prey and then throw its head up and toss the meat farther backwards into its mouth, like alligators and crocodiles.

- Despite the fierce jaws and strong features, Eryops probably waited for fish to become stranded at the water's edge or for a small reptile to walk into its deadly path.

- Footprints were found in carboniferous rocks, which showed that Eryops walked in short and broad strides. This probably meant that they found walking very slow and difficult.

Dinosaur Data

PRONUNCIATION:	**AR**-EE-OPS
SUBORDER:	EUSKELIA
FAMILY:	ERYOPIDAE
DESCRIPTION:	ALLIGATOR-LIKE AMPHIBIAN
FEATURES:	SMALL YET POWERFUL
DIET:	FISH, SMALL REPTILES AND AMPHIBIANS

GERROTHORAX

Ancient type of amphibian

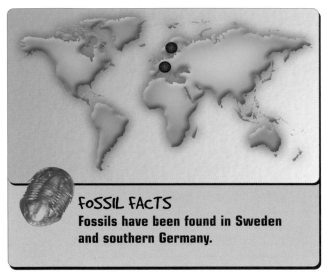

FOSSIL FACTS
Fossils have been found in Sweden and southern Germany.

Appearance

Gerrothorax was a type of **plagiosaurid**. This aquatic animal was thought to be 1 m (3 ft) long – that's about the same length as an adult seal. Gerrothorax looked a lot like a giant tadpole, but its body was flatter. Its head was short and wide and it had two small eyes that were really close together in the middle of its head.

Gerrothorax was not a dinosaur. It was an ancient type of amphibian that lived during the late Triassic period, about 200 million years ago. An amphibian is a kind of animal that is born from eggs, has bones and grows four legs. As babies they live in water and can then go on land. A frog is an amphibian.

Gerrothorax was a larval-like amphibian that lived in streams and lakes. Unlike frogs, it probably never left the water.

Like frogs, Gerrothorax had webbed feet. This was just on its back feet, probably to help propel it through the water. Gerrothorax also had a small tail.

Modern amphibians lose their gills when they grow older, Gerrothorax didn't. It had three pairs of gills throughout its life, meaning that it could live in water even as an adult.

Predators and diet

Gerrothorax was a meat eater and probably lay at the bottom of lakes, attracting prey with its mouth wide open, ready to catch whatever came swimming towards it. However, because of the flat head, it probably couldn't quickly snap its jaws as many fish do.

Gerrothorax may have had its own predators, which might explain why it was armoured above and below. Because of this heavy armour, it probably couldn't move very quickly.

MEGA FACTS

- Because its eyes were very close set on the top of its head, Gerrothorax could only look upwards so it would not have been able to see anything swimming underneath it.

- The very wide skull extended so much that it looked as if it had wings at each side.

Dinosaur Data

PRONUNCIATION:	GEH-ROH-**THOR**-AX
SUBORDER:	TREMATOSAURIA
FAMILY:	PLAGIOSAURIDAE
DESCRIPTION:	ANCIENT AMPHIBIAN
FEATURES:	FLAT, TADPOLE-LIKE BODY
DIET:	PROBABLY FISH

DIMETRODON
Four-footed sail-finned predator

Dimetrodon had two different kinds of teeth – shearing teeth and sharp canines or incisors. This is one of the features of Dimetrodon that marks it out as an early synapsid (see page 208). The only surviving synapsids are mammals, a group which includes humans.

Appearance

Whilst its two kinds of teeth was one of the most important features of Dimetrodon, one of its most obvious features was the large sail-like fin that grew from its back. This fin could be up to 1 m (3 ft) high at its tallest point and was supported by a series of spines that grew out from the vertebrae of Dimetrodon's spinal cord.

FOSSIL FACTS
Dimetrodon fossils have been found in the USA.

Dimetrodon was a **pelycosaur** and lived several tens of millions of years before the earliest dinosaurs. The name Dimetrodon was given by Edward Drinker Cope in 1884 and means 'two measures teeth'.

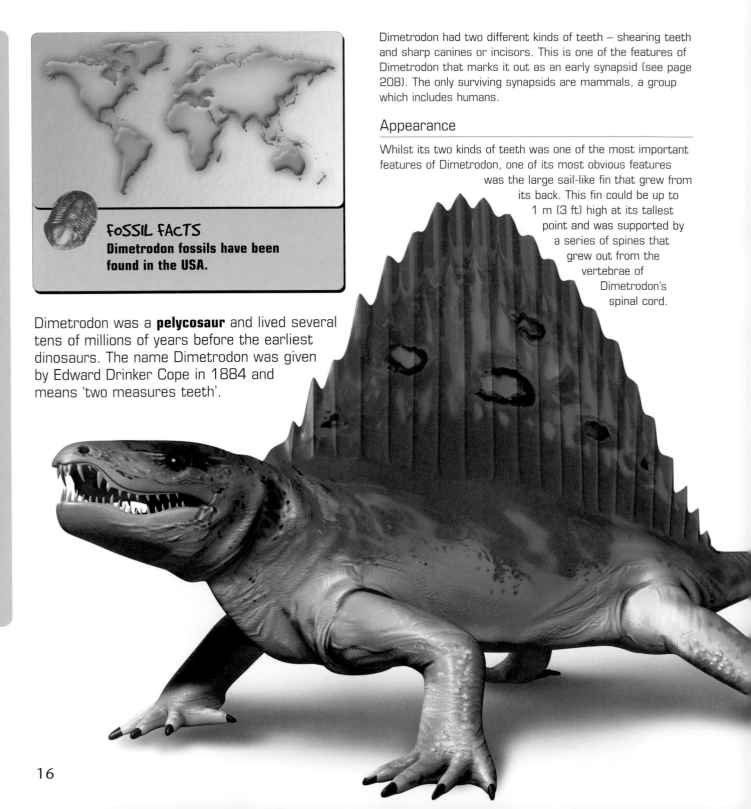

| Carboniferous period (350-300 million years ago) | Permian period (300-248 million years ago) | Triassic period (248-176 million years ago) | Jurassic period (176-130 million years ago) | |

The fin could be used to control the heat of the body (a thermo-regulator) as well as being used to attract a mate or frightening other species by making them appear larger and more ferocious. It may have been brightly or multi-coloured but we can't be certain (as with many creatures we have discovered as fossils) because we can't tell what patterns or colours their skin as this detail simply doesn't exist in the fossils.

Diet

Dimetrodon lived mostly in swampy areas. Fossilised skeletons indicate that this creature could grow to about 3.5 m (11ft 6in.) long and probably weighed about 250 kg (550 lb), making it a ferocious predator compared to the other creatures of its time (the largest creature in the Permian period is believed to have been the Moschops, a 5 m (16.5 ft) long **herbivore**).

Built for speed

It is believed that Dimetrodon would have been the dominant **carnivore** in its environment, sitting at the top of the food chain with no predators. Dimetrodon had a long tail, a large head and four legs that sprawled out to the sides of its body, unlike dinosaurs whose legs were underneath their bodies. It's thought that this arrangement combined with its muscles made Dimetrodon a fast runner, enabling it to run down other slower moving creatures such as Eryops (see page 12).

MEGA FACTS

- **Dimetrodon's large sail-like fin was an excellent heat-exchanger.**

- **Dimetrodon is believed to have been a dominant carnivore with no predators.**

The first Dimetrodon fossil was discovered in 1887.

Dinosaur Data

PRONUNCIATION:	DIE-**MET**-ROE-DON
SUBORDER:	SPHENACODONTIA
FAMILY:	SPHENACODONTIDAE
DESCRIPTION:	LARGE CARNIVORE
FEATURES:	LARGE SAIL-LIKE FIN, 4 SIDE-SPRAWLING LEGS, LARGE HEAD WITH TWO TYPES OF TEETH, LONG TAIL
DIET:	OTHER PELYCOSAURS, INSECTS AND ANIMALS

EDAPHOSAURUS

Land-living reptile

ANCESTORS OF THE DINOSAURS

FOSSIL FACTS
Fossils of this creature have been found in Europe and North America.

Appearance

Edophosaurus looked similar to Dimetrodon (see page 16) because of its spiny back. This spine looked like a sail along its back. The sail was supported by bones in the vertebral column and scientists aren't sure what the sail was used for. Some believe that it was used to help the animal warm itself up more quickly. Others believe that it was used to attract a mate or warn others.

The word Edaphosaurus means 'Earth lizard' in Greek. This reptile lived on land during the late Carboniferous and early Permian period, about 320 to 258 million years ago. This was a long time before the dinosaurs lived.

Edaphosaurus was a primitive **herbivore**. In fact, it was one of the earliest known plant-eating animals. It had flat teeth so it had to eat plants that it could easily crush. It probably lived near lakes or swamps.

It had a small, short and shallow skull and large eyes, with a wide body and thick tail. It was a **quadruped**. This quadruped was about 3.2 m (11 ft) long and weighed about 300 kg (660 lb).

We still know very little about the Edaphosaurus, as the only fossils that have ever been found only consist of a few fragments of its skeleton, including some of its spines.

Like the Dimetrodon, the Edaphosaurus was a **pelycosaur**. Pelycosaurs were small lizard-like animals that evolved into much larger and very different types. Some of the types were meat eaters and some were plant eaters like the Edophosaurus.

Pelycosaurs became extinct at beginning of the Permian period, long before the Triassic period when the dinosaurs evolved. Some of the types developed the sails on their backs and some did not. Eventually the synapsids evolved into the therapsids, which later led to the mammals.

MEGA FACTS

- In the morning, if Edaphosaurus stood with its sail at right angles to the rising sun, it would absorb the warmth quite quickly. This would raise Edaphosaurus' body temperature so that it could get going and find food quite quickly during the day.

- If it got too hot then by standing in a cooling breeze it could cool itself down quickly and effectively.

- Although nobody knows what colour its sail actually was it was thought to have been brightly-coloured and may have been used to attract a mate as some brightly-coloured birds do today.

- Although it could chew its food it also had a very large gut so it would swallow large amounts of partly-chewed leaves and stems and they would ferment in its gut to release the goodness.

Dinosaur Data

PRONUNCIATION:	AH-**DAF**-OH-**SAW**-US
SUBORDER:	PELYCOSAURIA
FAMILY:	EDAPHOSAURIDAE
DESCRIPTION:	A PRIMITIVE HERBIVORE
FEATURES:	SMALL AND STRONG
DIET:	PLANTS

19

WHAT ARE DINOSAURS?

Dinosaurs were a kind of prehistoric reptile. They ruled the Earth for more than 150 million years, during a period of time called the Mesozoic era. The first dinosaur appeared on Earth about 230 million years ago. They all died out about 65 million years ago.

Everything we know about the dinosaurs comes from the fossilised remains of their bones (and sometimes impressions of their skin, or footprints). This means scientists have very little to go on when they try to work out how dinosaurs lived. We cannot tell from fossils what colour a dinosaur's skin was, or what their voices sounded like. It is hard to tell how they

Some dinosaur myths

All dinosaurs were huge

Many were middle-sized or small. The smallest known dinosaur is Compsognathus (see page 62), which was only the size of a chicken.

All giant pre-historic animals were dinosaurs

Many other types of animal shared the Mesozoic era with the dinosaurs.
Pterosaurs flew, and marine reptiles like the ichthyosaurs swam in the oceans.

Some dinosaurs could fly, or swim

All dinosaurs lived on land. The pterosaurs and ichthyosaurs were not dinosaurs. Many scientists think that dinosaurs did eventually fly, though – by evolving into birds!

Dinosaurs were the biggest animals that ever lived

Although a plant-eating dinosaur called Argentinosaurus (see page 96) was the largest ever land animal, it was not as massive as a modern day giant, the blue whale.

Scientists have named about 800 kinds of dinosaurs so far and there must be many more fossils to find. New finds are made today almost every month – of course, not all of these are new species.

Most dinosaurs laid eggs and were cold-blooded. Apart from that, they were widely different in size, shape and speed. Some were **herbivores** and some **carnivores**. Some moved on all fours (these are called **quadrupeds**) and some on just their back legs (these are called **bipeds**).

behaved. Scientific detectives called **palaeontologists** study the fossil remains to learn as much as they can.

The name dinosaur means 'terrible lizard'. It comes from two Greek words: *deinos*, (terrifying) and *sauros* (lizard). The name was invented by Sir Richard Owen in 1842 (above left). Before that, people did not realise dinosaurs had once existed.

MEGA FACTS

- **Largest – Argentinosaurus, 35–45m (14–13 in.) long**

- **Smallest – Compsognathus, weighed 5.5kg (12 lb), and was only 60 cm (24 in.) long**

- **Widest – Ankylosaurus, 1.5 m (5 ft) wide**

- **Longest neck – Mamenchisaurus, neck was 10 m (33 ft) long**

- **Fastest – Ornithomiminee, ran at 64–85 km/ph (40–53 mph)**

- **First discovered – Iguanodon, found 1822**

- **Oldest – Eoraptor, lived 227 million years ago**

TRIASSIC PERIOD

Eoraptor

Roughly 248 million years ago, about 95% of all species died out, including many marine animals. The cause might have been global cooling, volcanic eruptions, or a decrease in the continental shelf area during the formation of Pangaea. This catastrophic extinction and continental rearrangement opened the way for the rise of the dinosaurs and mammals.

The Triassic period was the first part of the **Mesozoic era**, the Age of Dinosaurs. It lasted from about 248 to 206 million years ago. During this period, dinosaurs and mammals evolved.

Coral bed

Climate

There was no polar ice during this time, and the temperature was constantly warm. The continents were jammed together, forming the supercontinent **Pangaea**.

The formation of Pangaea, 220 million years ago, decreased the amount of shoreline, formed mountains, and gave the interior of the supercontinent a dry, desert-like terrain. The polar regions were moist and temperate. The climate was generally hot and dry, with strong seasonality.

Living things

There were no dinosaurs at the beginning of the period, but there were many amphibians, and some reptiles and dicynodonts (like Lystrosaurus). During the early Triassic period, corals appeared and ammonites recovered from the Permian extinction. Seed plants dominated the land.

Ammonite fossil

Mammals appear

During the late Triassic period, 220 million years ago, the first mammals appeared. Some scientists believe that mammals evolved from a group of extinct mammal-like reptiles, Theriodontia, which were therapsids. These primitive mammals were tiny and are thought to have been nocturnal.

Early dinosaurs

The very earliest dinosaurs were small, two-legged meat eaters, such as Coelophysis (see page 86) and Eoraptor (see page 84).

Eoraptor was a small, primitive, meat-eating dinosaur with sharp teeth.

The first plant eaters were prosaurapods like Massospondylus and Plateosaurus.

They could walk on two or four legs, presumably rearing up to get at higher plant life. Although they were small in comparison to the size of the later giant plant-eating dinosaurs, the prosauropods were by far the largest land animals of their time.

The rise of the dinosaurs during the late Triassic led to the decline of other, previously successful animal groups. Many sprawling reptiles and amphibians disappeared, and so did advanced mammal-like reptiles.

Late Triassic extinction

The Triassic period ended with a mass extinction accompanied by huge volcanic eruptions about 208–213 million years ago. The supercontinent Pangaea began to break apart. Roughly 35% of all animal families died out. Most of the early, primitive dinosaurs also became extinct, but other, more adaptive dinosaurs evolved in the Jurassic period.

No one is certain what caused this late Triassic extinction. Some possibilities include global cooling or an asteroid impact. This extinction allowed the dinosaurs to expand into many parts that were now unoccupied. Dinosaurs would become increasingly dominant, and remained that way for the next 150 million years.

Plateosaurus

23

JURASSIC PERIOD

After the Triassic period came the Jurassic period, which lasted from about 206 to 144 million years ago. Huge, long-necked dinosaurs appeared during the Jurassic period.

There was a minor mass extinction roughly 190–183 million years ago in which more than 80% of marine life (like many clams) and many other shallow-water species died out. The cause of this extinction is unknown.

In the middle of this period, the supercontinent Pangaea started to drift apart. A north-south rift formed and, by the late Jurassic period, Pangaea was split in two by huge rifts on the Earth's surface that created two new land areas, Laurasia in the north and Gondwana in the south. There must have been some land bridges between the two new supercontinents, because skeletons of dinosaurs have been found at opposite ends of the country from each other.

Allosaurus

Climate

At the beginning of the Jurassic period, the climate was hot and dry, but, when Pangaea began to break up, there were vast flooded areas, tropical forests, and coral reefs. The breakup of the land and the creation of large seas affected the global climate.

New dinosaurs

The tropical plant life which grew over huge areas brought about new dinosaurs, such as the sauropods like Apatosaurus (see page 100), Diplodocus (see page 98) and Brachiosaurus (see page 94).

Their long necks gave them access to the higher tree-top plants that other dinosaurs could not reach.

Apatosaurus

Stegosaurus

Diplodocus

Many new groups also appeared. Meat-eating theropods like Allosaurus (see page 72) and Compsognathus (see page 62), and plated plant eaters like Stegosaurus (see page 116), evolved. Smaller coelurosaurs like Coelurus (see page 85) and Ornitholestes hunted lizards, mammals, and insects.

Sea life

In the Jurassic seas, there were abundant coral reefs, fish, ichthyosaurs (fish-like reptiles), giant marine crocodiles, and sharks. The air was dominated by the pterosaurs, the flying reptiles from the same original archosaur group as the dinosaurs. These were the largest vertebrates ever known to fly. Archaeopteryx also appeared, the earliest known bird, with many dinosaur features, proving that birds evolved from dinosaurs.

In terms of sheer size and geography, the Jurassic period is the high point of the dinosaur era. The upright way of walking allowed the dinosaurs to develop different body shapes and sizes to take full advantage of the environment. By the end of the period, dinosaurs had expanded to fill virtually almost every usable part of the land surface.

There was a minor mass extinction toward the end of the period. During this extinction, most of the stegosaurid and enormous sauropod dinosaurs died out. No one knows what caused this extinction.

25

CRETACEOUS PERIOD

The Cretaceous period, lasting from 144 to 65 million years ago, was the last part of the Mesozoic era. Most of the known dinosaurs lived during the Cretaceous period. During this time, mammals flourished; flowering plants evolved and changed the landscape radically. There was a high level of tectonic activity (continental plate movement) and accompanying volcanic activity.

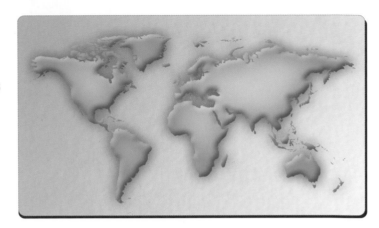

The Cretaceous period ended 65 million years ago with the extinction of the dinosaurs and many other prehistoric life forms. This mass extinction was the second most extensive in the history of the earth.

Geography and climate change

The break-up of the supercontinent **Pangaea** into separate continents was underway. By the end of the period the outlines of continents were roughly those that we recognise today. In the first half of the Cretaceous period, temperatures were warm and global sea levels were high.

During the mid-Cretaceous period, many mountain ranges were formed, including California's Sierra Nevadas, the Rocky Mountains in the western USA, and the European Alps. The sea levels rose, covering about one-third of the land area.

Towards the end of the period, there was a drop in sea level, causing greater temperature extremes. At the end of the Cretaceous period, there were severe climate changes, lowered sea levels, and high volcanic activity.

Rocky mountains, USA

Cretaceous dinosaurs

We know of more different species from the late Cretaceous Period than we do from all the other dinosaur periods put together. Huge carnivores like Tyrannosaurus Rex (see page 54) and Giganotosaurus (see page 56) appeared, as did Triceratops (see page 136) and many others.

There was a tremendous diversity in dinosaur species. The effect of the land breakup, as well as new plant life in the form of flowering plants (angiosperms), meant that dinosaurs started to become isolated from each other on separate continents. The same species of dinosaurs developed in different ways, depending on the areas they lived in. For example, there were noticeable differences between the North American hadrosaurs and the groups in China or Africa.

Other cretaceous life

Mammals were flourishing during this period, and many creatures such as snakes and moths appeared.

Flowering plants, like magnolia, developed and radically changed the landscape. The earliest fossils of birds resembling pelicans, flamingos, and sandpipers were from the Cretaceous period.

Mass extinction

At the end of the Cretaceous period, about 65 million years ago, a mass extinction wiped out the dinosaurs (except for the birds) and many other animals. The primary cause of the extinction is thought to be an asteroid impact, but there are a lot of other theories, including volcanoes and climate changes due to continental drift (see page 10). Although this extinction was huge, it was small when compared to the extinction which preceded the existence of the dinosaurs. The age of reptiles came to an end; the age of mammals was about to begin.

DINOSAUR BRAINS

Some scientists believe that dinosaurs were dull, stupid creatures, and whilst this might be partially true for the large plant eaters, this was not the case for the smaller, highly-active predators who had to think and move quickly in order to capture enough prey to stay alive. Luckily dinosaurs had tough, bony skulls which meant that their skulls were well preserved, and we can find out about their brains.

Small brains

Some of the slow plant eaters, like Apatosaurus (see page 100), had giant bodies but tiny brains. For example, Stegosaurus (see page 116) had a brain the size of a walnut that weighed just 70 g (3 oz). In relation to its size, Stegosaurus had the smallest brain of any dinosaur. However, Stegosaurus also had a secondary nerve centre (sometimes incorrectly called a second brain) near the base of its spine that helped it move its rear legs and tail.

These dinosaurs belonged to a group called the **sauropods** that didn't need much of a brain to survive. All they had to do was eat plants — they didn't have to hunt for food or look out for predators. Another **herbivore**, Triceratops (a horned dinosaur or **ceratopsian**), only had a 300 g (12 oz) brain in a body of 6,000–9,000 kg (6–9 tons).

More intelligent dinosaurs

Dinosaurs which lived in herds, such as the plant-eating hadrosaurs (see page 104), survived through herd communication and so used their brains much more. It is thought that some hadrosaurs, such as Parasaurolophus (see page 180), were able to use their distinctive head crests as sound-making devices, blowing air through the internal tubes to produce a noise. This would have been ideal as an alarm to the herd when a predator was spotted.

Hadrosaurs also had no armour, so were much more intelligent as they constantly had to be on the lookout for danger from predators.

Parasaurolophus

28

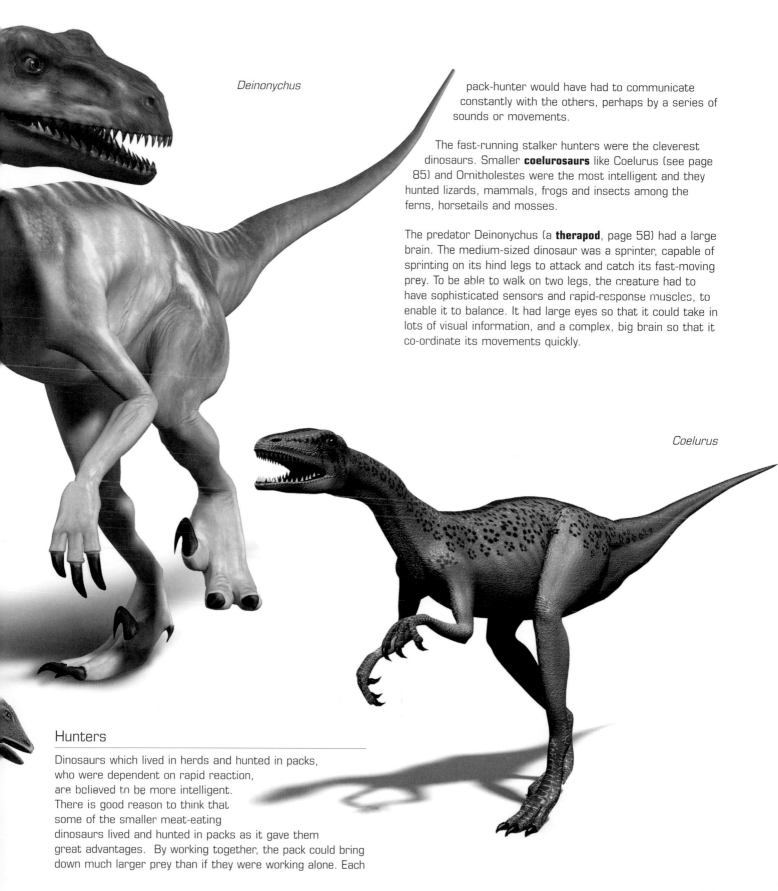

Deinonychus

pack-hunter would have had to communicate constantly with the others, perhaps by a series of sounds or movements.

The fast-running stalker hunters were the cleverest dinosaurs. Smaller **coelurosaurs** like Coelurus (see page 85) and Ornitholestes were the most intelligent and they hunted lizards, mammals, frogs and insects among the ferns, horsetails and mosses.

The predator Deinonychus (a **therapod**, page 58) had a large brain. The medium-sized dinosaur was a sprinter, capable of sprinting on its hind legs to attack and catch its fast-moving prey. To be able to walk on two legs, the creature had to have sophisticated sensors and rapid-response muscles, to enable it to balance. It had large eyes so that it could take in lots of visual information, and a complex, big brain so that it co-ordinate its movements quickly.

Coelurus

Hunters

Dinosaurs which lived in herds and hunted in packs, who were dependent on rapid reaction, are believed to be more intelligent. There is good reason to think that some of the smaller meat-eating dinosaurs lived and hunted in packs as it gave them great advantages. By working together, the pack could bring down much larger prey than if they were working alone. Each

SENSES

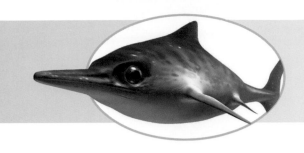

Saurornithoides

page 54) and Giganotosaurus (see page 56), the largest meat-eating dinosaur of all time, had a keen sense of smell and good eyesight. They could possibly have smelt potential prey from some distance away. They could also pick up the scent of dead bodies, from a long distance, from which they could scavenge meat.

It is thought that some dinosaurs' noses had a special scent gland that would have been used to release hormones into the air. The hormones could have been carried lomg distance and may have been used to attract a mate.

It is hard to tell what dinosaurs were like because humans haven't been able to watch them and observe how they behave, but scientists can work out information about their senses from evidence left behind. Like all living things, dinosaurs had five senses; taste, touch, sight, sound and smell.

Touch

A dinosaur's sense of touch was probably not very well developed, because of their thick skin. Their sense of taste was more well developed, although big eaters like Allosaurus (see page 72) probably didn't taste much of their meal when eating as they eat so fast!

Taste and smell

The senses of taste and smell were controlled by the same part of the dinosaur's brain, and were closely linked. They were used by hunters and hunted to keep track of each other, by some plant eaters to tell the difference between certain foods and, in many species, as part of the mating process.

The predators were probably able to smell very well, in order to hunt their prey. Both Tyrannosaurus Rex (see

Troodon

Vision and hearing

Most dinosaurs had good side vision, with eyes set at the sides of their heads, but because their eyes didn't face forward, they weren't very good at judging distances. Smaller meat-eating dinosaurs had good vision and good co-ordination, which meant they were very successful in stalking and chasing smaller creatures.

Troodon (see page 82) had exceptionally large eyes, based on the size of the eye sockets, and the biggest brain of any dinosaur relative to its body size.

Coelophysis (see page 86), a small meat-eating **therapod** dinosaur, had a large brain in comparison to its reptilian ancestors, and its senses were finely tuned. It had excellent eyesight and hearing that, in combination with its fast legs, long neck, short arms and sharp claws, would have helped it catch fish, small reptiles and other prey.

Dinosaurs did not have exterior ear flaps like mammals but heard through holes set far back in the head behind their eyes. It was probably herding dinosaurs, with their strong need to communicate, that had the most acute sense of hearing. Hadrosaurs (see page 104) display the only real evidence so far of being able to make noises, with a variety of nasal trumpets and air sacs. However, like many modern land animals, dinosaurs would probably have made noises if they needed to, for example to attract a mate, defend their territory or warn of danger.

Giganotosaurus

HEADS AND TAILS

Every dinosaur was made up of the same basic skeletal parts, but heads and tails varied in appearance and function.

The biggest dinosaurs often had very small heads. A Brachiosaurus (see page 94) may have eaten up to a tonne of plants every day just to stay alive. It had a head not much larger than a horse's and teeth which didn't chew. Torosaurus was also a **herbivore** but had the most powerful jaw muscles of any known dinosaur. These, when combined with its sharp beak and around 600 teeth, allowed it to slice through any plant, including tree branches.

Skills

The skull differed from dinosaur to dinosaur, depending on what it was needed for. Deinonychus (see page 58) had a lightweight skull.

Combined with its slim neck, this was ideal for quick, snapping bites. Tyrannosaurus Rex (see page 54), had a large head which was heavily reinforced with bone and shock-absorbing muscle to withstand the impact of crashing into a victim with mouth open and then delivering a crushing bite. Its jaw could be 1.2 m (4 ft) long and the many teeth would attack an animal. It had to swallow its food whole, and could probably gulp up to 70 kg (154 lb) of meat in one go.

Styracosaurus

Deinonychus skull

Dinosaurs had different markings and body parts to distinguish them from each other, compete with other males and find a mate. Styracosaurus (see page 150) had an impressive head structure. Its round bony frill was actually longer than the skull itself, and decorated round the outer edge with long spikes. By tilting its head forward and swinging it from side to side, Styracosaurus could produce an impressive display of size and aggression to frighten off other males and display their strength.

Protecting the head and neck

As the head and neck were such a vulnerable part for a dinosaur, it was important that it could be protected. Some dinosaurs, such as Euoplocephalus, had studs and plates to protect them. Its head was heavily armoured, with slabs of reinforcing bone over all exposed surfaces and triangular side studs above and below the eyes. The eyelids were made of bone, closing like steel shutters, to deflect the gouging claw of an attacker.

Tails

The end of Diplodocus' tail was so long and thin that some scientists believe it was used like a bullwhip for defence. Although quite a few **saurapod** tracks have been found around the world, there are very few that show evidence of tail-drag marks. Scientists have decided that the saurapods kept their tails up off the ground when they walked.

Ankylosaurus (see page 118), had a heavily-armoured tail. Ankylosaurus, if attacked, could use its club-like tail as a weapon, swinging it from side to side like a knight's mace. The club itself was a weighty mass of fused bony tissue that was quite capable of smashing through the leg bones of even the largest dinosaurs.

Tyrannosaurus Rex skull

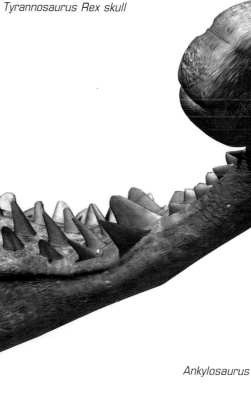

Ankylosaurus

ICHTHYOSAURUS

Aquatic hunter/killer

DINOSAURS IN THE SEA

Ichthyosaurus evolved from reptiles, but could swim like fish. It swam by moving its powerful tails from side to side. Since it needed to breathe air periodically, it probably lived close to the surface of the sea. It breathed through nostrils on the top of the head, near the top of the snout. Its long snout was packed with conical, pointed teeth.

FOSSIL FACTS

Ichthyosaurus fossils have been found in England, Germany, Greenland and Canada. The first was found in England in the early 19th century.

Appearance

Ichthyosaurus means 'fish lizard'. It was named in 1818 by Charles König from the British Museum. It is not a true dinosaur but a dolphin-like marine reptile. Ichthyosaurus lived from the early Jurassic period to the early Cretaceous period – around 206 to 140 million years ago.

Reproduction and diet

Ichthyosaurus was smooth-skinned and streamlined, and had limbs (flippers) like large paddles to balance it in the water – the front 'paddles' were twice as large as the back ones. Its eyes were unusually large, and surrounded by a strong ring of bone. A fish-like tail helped propel it, and a dorsal fin provided extra balance.

Ichthyosaurus gave birth to live young – we know this because fossils have been found showing baby Ichthyosaurus bones in the abdomen of adults. Fossils have also helped us learn about the diet of Ichthyosaurus – the hard hooks found on the tentacles of squid cannot be digested and so remained in the belly; one fossil of an Ichthyosaurus showed it had swallowed at least 1,500 squid while alive.

The first complete ichthyosaurus fossil remains were found at Lyme Regis in England, by a girl called Mary Anning, in the early 19th century. Mary Anning made a living from collecting, studying and selling fossils.

MEGA FACTS

- Most were around 2 m (6 ft) long, though some were as big as 9 m (30 ft). An average weight for these dolphin-like creatures was 90 kg (200 lb).

- We know Ichthyosaurus must have moved fast to hunt its prey, because the remains of a fast-swimming fish called Pholidophorus have been found in fossilised Ichthyosaurus droppings. It could swim at speeds of up to 40 km/h (25 mph).

- Ichthyosaurus skeletons found at Holzmaden (Germany) were so well preserved that scientists could see outlines of skin as well as bones.

- In 2000, an Ichthyosaurus skeleton, believed to be almost a perfect specimen, was revealed as a fake when it was cleaned. It had been made in the Victorian age from the bones of two different creatures and some bones made out of plaster.

Icthyosaurus fossil

Dinosaur Data

PRONUNCIATION:	IK-THEE-OH-**SAWR**-US
SUBORDER:	ICHTHYOSAURIA
FAMILY:	ICHTHYOSAURIDAE
DESCRIPTION:	OCEAN-DWELLING PREDATOR
FEATURES:	ENORMOUS EYES, FOUR CRESCENT-SHAPED FLIPPERS, DORSAL FIN
DIET:	FISH, OCTOPUS AND OTHER SEA-DWELLING CREATURES

ELASMOSAURUS

Long-necked marine reptile

DINOSAURS IN THE SEA

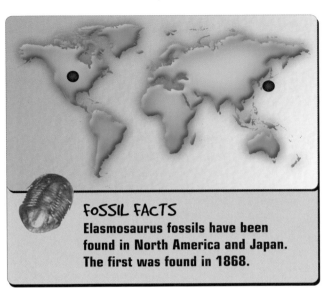

FOSSIL FACTS
Elasmosaurus fossils have been found in North America and Japan. The first was found in 1868.

Elasmosaurus means 'thin-plated lizard' – the name refers to the plate-like bones in the creature's pelvic girdle. It lived 88–65 million years ago, and swam in the great inland sea that covered much of the western part of North America in those times. Its body was dwarfed by its long thin neck and shorter tail.

Elasmosaurus was named by Edward Drinker Cope, who discovered the first fossil.

Unfortunately, when Cope assembled his Elasmosaurus skeleton for display, he placed the head on the wrong end! His rivals soon pointed out his mistake, and made fun of him for it for the rest of his career.

Appearance

The neck of Elasmosaurus contained more than 70 **vertebrae**. Elasmosaurus was the largest of a type of marine reptile called **plesiosaurs**. It had a large body, four long, broad paddles for limbs, and a small head with sharp, interlocking teeth.

The long neck may have enabled Elasmosaurus to feed in a number of different ways.

Dinosaur Data

PRONUNCIATION:	EE-**LAZ**-MOH-SAWR-US
SUBORDER:	PLESIOSAURIOID
FAMILY:	ELASMOSAURIDAE
DESCRIPTION:	HUGE, SLOW-SWIMMING MARINE REPTILE
FEATURES:	EXTREMELY LONG NECK, TINY HEAD
DIET:	FISH AND OTHER SMALL MARINE CREATURES

It may have floated along on the surface, stretching down to the sea bottom to catch fish and other marine creatures. It could also make attacks upward at shoals of fish while its body was much lower down in the water. It could move slowly and stealthily toward them, then attack with a quick darting movement. The small size of its head and its narrow neck meant it could only eat and swallow smaller creatures. Elasmosaurus fossils have been found with rounded pebbles in their stomachs – perhaps they swallowed these to aid their digestion or to help them sink further down into the water.

Elasmosaurus is believed to have been a very slow swimmer. It would have travelled long distances to find safe mating and breeding grounds.

Reproduction

For a long time, it was assumed that Elasmosaurus laid eggs like most reptiles, crawling ashore to lay its eggs on land. However, many scientists now think that Elasmosaurus gave birth to live young, which it raised until they could look after themselves in the predator-filled ocean. Elasmosaurus may have travelled together in small groups to protect their young.

MEGA FACTS

- About 14 m (46 ft) long, Elasmosaurus was the longest of the plesiosaurs.

- Pictures often show Elasmosaurus holding its head high above the surface of the water at the end of its long neck. Actually, gravity would have made it impossible for it to lift much more than its head above water.

- Elasmosaurus, with its long snake-like neck, is one of the candidates for the Loch Ness Monster (see page 228).

37

KRONOSAURUS

Giant short-necked marine reptile

Kronosaurus means 'Kronos's lizard'. It had a short neck, four flippers, a huge head with powerful jaws and a short, pointed tail.

Kronosaurus was a marine reptile called a pliosaur (a type of **plesiosaur**). It was heavier, faster and fiercer than most plesiosaurs. It lived in the seas that covered parts of Australia, and breathed air. It swam with four powerful paddle-like flippers and may have been able to climb out onto land and move around a little. It probably had to leave water to lay its eggs in nests it would dig in the sand.

Diet

Kronosaurus ate other sea creatures such as ammonites and squid. Rounded teeth at the back of its powerful jaws enabled Kronosaurus to crunch up tough shells and crush bone.

The fossilised remains of turtles and even smaller plesiosaurs have been found in the stomachs of Kronosaurus fossils, and long-necked plesiosaur skeletons have been found with Kronosaurus-like toothmarks on the bones. Like Elasmosaurus (see page 36), small stones have been found in Kronosaurus stomachs which might have helped them grind up their food during digestion.

Kronosaurus skeleton

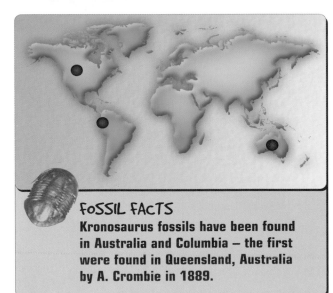

FOSSIL FACTS
Kronosaurus fossils have been found in Australia and Columbia — the first were found in Queensland, Australia by A. Crombie in 1889.

Kronosaurus

Dinosaur Data

PRONUNCIATION:	CROW-NO-SAWR-US
DESCRIPTION:	POWERFUL AQUATIC PREDATOR
FEATURES:	HUGE HEAD, POWERFUL JAWS
DIET:	**CARNIVORE**; ATE OTHER MARINE CREATURES

Kronosaurus may have been able to 'scent' under water for its prey – it had internal nostrils where water could enter, and external ones further back on the top of its skull for water to exit. While the water passed from one set to the other, scent particles could be detected.

Appearance

Kronosaurus had an enormous head as skulls have been found measuring 3 m (10 ft). As their whole body length is believed to be only around

9 m (30 ft), this means their head took up a third of it!

It was originally thought to be much longer, earning it the title of 'largest ever plesiosaur', but recent studies have led scientists to downsize their image of Kronosaurus. The team of scientists who mounted the first specimen for display had to fill in many 'gaps' in the skeleton – they gave their mounted Kronosaurus too many vertebrae and so made it longer than it should have been.

MEGA FACTS

- Fast and fierce – one of the top predators of the ancient ocean.

- Some of Kronosaurus' teeth were 25 cm (10 in.) long, although much of this length was embedded in the jawbone.

- When Kronosaurus fossils were first discovered in 1889, they were believed to come from an ichthyosaur. Kronosaurus did not get a name of its own until 1924.

- When the first Kronosaurus skeleton was assembled, the specimen was in such a bad state that the team had to fill in many details using plaster and their own imagination. This led to the creature being nicknamed the 'Plasterosaurus'!

TYLOSAURUS

Gigantic marine predator

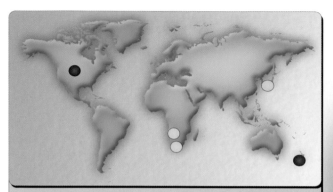

FOSSIL FACTS
Tylosaurus fossils have been found in North America and New Zealand. The first fossils were found in Kansas (USA) in 1869. The yellow dots show where material which may relate to Tylosaurus has also been found — in Angola, South Africa and Japan.

The name Tylosaurus comes from the Greek words *tylos* (knob or protuberance) and *sauros* (lizard). It is named after its remarkable long and almost cylindrical snout that has a rounded, bony end. Tylosaurus was a marine reptile known as a **mosasaur**. It was one of the most gigantic of the mosasaurs, growing up to 12 m (39 ft) long — that's as long as a double-decker bus!

Dinosaur Data

PRONUNCIATION:	**TIE**-LOW-**SAWR**-US
SUBORDER:	LACERTILIA
FAMILY:	MOSASAURIDAE
DESCRIPTION:	MASSIVE SEA PREDATOR
FEATURES:	POWERFUL TAIL, LONG ROUNDED SNOUT
DIET:	FISH, MARINE CREATURES, FLIGHTLESS BIRDS

Appearance

It had a long slender body with a long and powerful tail to propel it through the water. Most scientists think it propelled itself by moving its tail from side to side, just as a crocodile does. It had a long and massive head which was over 1 m (3 ft) long. Its four limbs were long, slim flippers. The bony tip at the end of its long narrow snout may have been used to ram and stun its prey, and to fight with other Tylosaurus. Its huge jaws contained masses of sharp cone-shaped teeth.

Like most mosasaurs, Tylosaurus probably had a forked tongue, the ability to 'smell' scent particles in water or air (like snakes), and large eyes (and so excellent eyesight).

MEGA FACTS

- Tylosaurus rarely bit off more than it could chew – it was able to flex its lower jaw, allowing it to open its mouth very wide and swallow large prey in one piece, just like a modern day snake.

- In 2002, a Tylosaurus skeleton went on display at the Alabama Museum of Natural History. It took an estimated 2,000 hours of work to recover and prepare this specimen.

- Tylosaurus not only had a bony bump on the end of its snout, but bony plates on its head and scales all over its body.

Diet

These giant sea hunters ate other sea creatures – fish, shellfish, smaller mosasaurs, turtles and even diving **pterandons** that dipped too close to the sea's surface!

Many different species of Tylosaurus have been named over the years, but scientists now recognise only a handful as valid. These are:

- Tylosaurus proriger
- Tylosaurus nepaeolicius
- Tylosaurus haummuriensis
- Tylosaurus kansasensis

MOSASAURUS

Giant aquatic predator

D
I
N
O
S
A
U
R
S

I
N

T
H
E

S
E
A

Mosasaurus is named after the River Meuse near Maastricht (Netherlands), where the first fossil specimen was found (*mosa-*, the Latin name for the Meuse River, and -*saurus* for lizard). It was given this name in 1822.

Mosasaurus was a gigantic meat-eating reptile that lived 70–65 million years ago. It frequented shallow seas, as it still needed to breathe air. It had a long, streamlined body, four paddle-like limbs, and a long, powerful tail. It was a powerful swimmer, between 12 m (39 ft) and 17.6 m (58 ft) in length. Its large head had huge jaws (up to 1.45 m (5 ft) long). These jaws could open up to 1 m (3 ft) thanks to the Mosasaurus' peculiar jaw design.

Dinosaur Data

PRONUNCIATION:	**MOES**-AH-**SAWR**-US
DESCRIPTION:	GIANT, SWIFT-MOVING AQUATIC PREDATOR
FEATURES:	SPECIALLY HINGED JAWS, LONG AND POWERFUL TAIL
DIET:	SHARKS, FISH AND OTHER MARINE REPTILES

FOSSIL FACTS
Fossils have been found in North America, Africa, New Zealand and Europe. The first Mosasaurus fossil was found in a quarry in the Netherlands in 1780.

Jaws

Mosasaurus had very special jaws. It had an extra joint halfway along the jaw, which let it handle huge mouthfuls of food. Its lower jaw could drop lower and also move out sideways – much like snakes which can 'unhinge' their jaws to swallow very large pieces of food like whole rats. Monitor lizards, to which Mosasaurus is directly related, still has this special jaw. Set into this jaw were rows of backward-curving teeth. Just as with sharks, when one tooth wore down, another grew in its place.

Diet

The preserved stomach contents of Mosasaur fossils show them to have eaten sharks, bony fish, turtles and other marine reptiles.

Skeleton

Mosasaurus had about 100 vertebrae in its back (four times as many as humans), each joined to the next by a flexible ball-and-socket joint. This would have allowed Mosasaurus to move in the water like an eel. It was one of the most ferocious aquatic predators of its time.

Reproduction

Scientists cannot agree as to whether Mosasaurus came up on land to lay its eggs in sand (like turtles), or gave birth to live young in the water.

Mosasaurus fossils were some of the earliest dinosaur fossils to be discovered, and because of them, scientists began to discuss the possibility that such fossils belonged to species which had actually died out.

MEGA FACTS

- Mosasaurus is directly related to monitor lizards.

- Recent studies suggest the first Mosasaurus specimen was actually a partial skull found as early as 1766, near St Pietersburg, near Maastricht.

- In 1795, a Mosasaurus skull was traded to the occupying French army for 600 bottles of wine! It sits in a Paris museum.

- Like a Tylosaurus, a Mosasaurus rarely bit off more than it could chew – it could unhinge its special jaw to swallow huge prey such as sharks.

Mosasaurus skeleton

OPHTHALMOSAURUS

Huge-eyed aquatic hunter

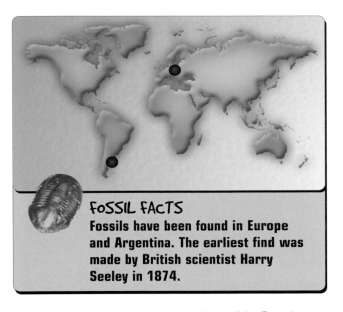

FOSSIL FACTS
Fossils have been found in Europe and Argentina. The earliest find was made by British scientist Harry Seeley in 1874.

Ophthalmosaurus means 'eye lizard' in Greek. The name comes from its dinner-plate sized eyes – Ophthalmosaurus had the largest eyes relative to its size of any vertebrate, measuring up to

23 cm (9 in.) across. These eyes took up almost the whole depth of its skull on each side. Fossil remains show a ring of strong bone surrounding these eyes – these would have supported the eye against water pressure, suggesting that Ophthalmosaurus could dive into deep, dark water after prey or to hide from predators.

It may well have been a night hunter, as its large eyes were well adapted for low light conditions and would have helped it to spot the squid that were its favourite prey. (Large eyes can house more light-gathering cells, and so are more effective in the dark.)

Appearance

Although it was perfectly adapted for living in the water, Ophthalmosaurus needed to breathe air, like a dolphin or whale does. It was not a true dinosaur,

Dinosaur Data

PRONUNCIATION:	OFF-**THAL**-MOH-**SAW**-RUS
FAMILY:	ICHTHYSAURIDAE
DESCRIPTION:	DOLPHIN-LIKE HUNTER
FEATURES:	ENORMOUS EYES
DIET:	SQUID AND FISH

but a marine reptile. Swift and supple, its 6 m (20 ft) long body resembled that of a dolphin, tear-shaped with a dorsal fin. Its front fins were more developed than its back ones; Ophthalmosaurus probably propelled itself with its tail and steered with its front fins. The skull took up about 1 m (3 ft) of its 6 m (20 ft) body.

The bends

Although it could dive to great depths, Ophthalmosaurus may have paid a price for doing so. Fossil evidence shows clear signs of what modern deep-sea divers call the bends – when a diver ascends too quickly, decompressed nitrogen in the blood forms painful bubbles that can damage tissue and even bone. Ophthalmosaurus remains show signs of the animal having suffered in exactly this way, leaving visible depressions in the joints and limb bones.

Reproduction

Ophthalmosaurus could not get onto land to lay eggs, instead giving birth to live young in the water. Their young – which we call 'pups' – were born tail first, to prevent them from drowning. We know this because fossils survive of females in the act of giving birth. Numbers of young ranged from two to 11, although it seems to have been most normal to give birth to only two or three at a time.

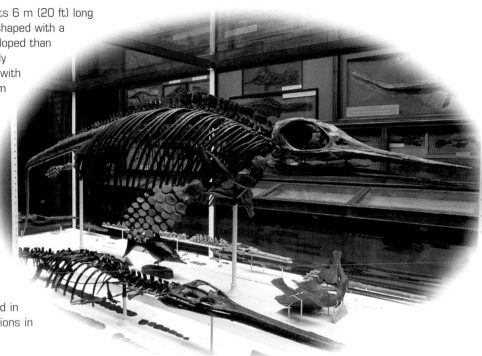

Ophthalmosaurus and Stenosaurus

MEGA FACTS

- Ophthalmosaurus lived 165–150 million years ago.

- May have been capable of diving to depths of 4.9 km (3 miles); calculations show it would still have had clear sight this far down.

- Had an almost toothless jaw, specially adapted for catching squid and fish.

PLESIOSAURUS

Four-paddled marine reptile

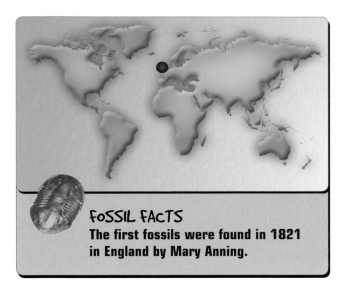

FOSSIL FACTS
The first fossils were found in 1821 in England by Mary Anning.

Plesiosaurus skeleton

The name Plesiosaurus means 'near to lizard' or 'near lizard' and comes from the Greek words *plesios* (near to) and *sauros* (lizard). The name was coined by H. T. De La Beche and William D. Conybeare in 1821.

Appearance

Plesiosaurus was one of a number of marine reptiles that lived at the same time as the dinosaurs. Plesiosaurus was characterised by long, thin neck, tiny head and wide bodies. Plesiosaurus was about 2.3 m (7 ft 6 in.) long and may have weighed around 90 kg (198 lb).

Plesiosaurus lived in the open oceans but still needed to breathe air, this means it would had to have come to the surface regularly to breathe – much like whales and dolphins do.

We believe it swam using its four flippers in pairs, one pair 'rowing' and the other pair moving in an up-down motion with the tail being used for steering. No other creatures are known to swim in this way.

Reproduction

Scientists had speculated that, like the turtle, it dragged itself up onto sandy beaches to lay its eggs, which it would bury in the sand before heading back to the ocean again.

However, the current theory is that the Plesiosaurus gave birth to live young in the oceans. This would certainly have made things easier on the baby Plesiosaurus as it wouldn't have to hatch and then scurry down the beach to reach the relative safety of the ocean like baby sea turtles.

Diet

Fossilised remains found in the stomachs of Plesiosaurus fossils show that they ate fish and other swimming animals. We know they also swallowed small stones! We believe this was either to help to break up their food or to help weight them down for diving deeper into the ocean.

The first Plesiosaurus fossils were found on the **Jurassic Coast**. In 2004 a fully intact fossilised juvenile Plesiosaurus was found about 50 km (31 miles) north of where the first Plesiosaurus was found!

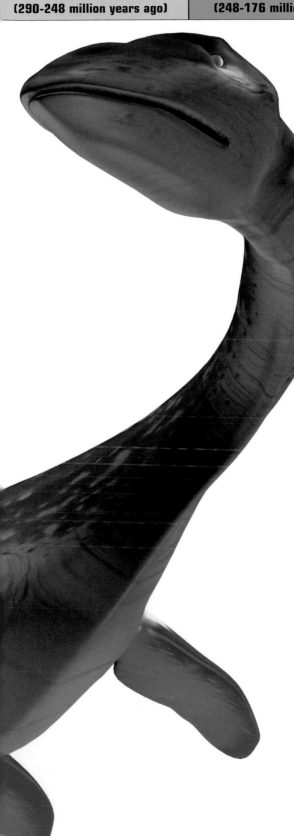

MEGA FACTS

- The first Plesiosaurus fossil was found long before the first dinosaur fossil was found.

- A Plesiosaurus is one of the creatures mentioned in Jules Verne's *Journey to the Centre of the Earth* – it battles an Icthyosaur (see page 34).

- Many people believe that the Loch Ness Monster (see page 228) could be a Plesiosaurus. However, this seems unlikely as the cold water of the loch would not support a cold-blooded creature like the Plesiosaurus and the loch only formed 10,000 years ago – whilst Plesiosaurus became extinct millions of years ago.

Dinosaur Data

PRONUNCIATION:	**PLEE**-SEE-O-**SAWR**-UHS
SUBORDER:	PLESIOSAUROID
FAMILY:	PLESIOSAURIDAE
DESCRIPTION:	ROUGHLY MAN-SIZED AQUATIC PREDATOR
FEAUTURES:	LONG SINUOUS NECK, FOUR PADDLE LIKE FINS, TINY HEAD WITH LONG SHARP TEETH
DIET:	FISH AND SMALLER AQUATIC ANIMALS

NOTHOSAURUS

Paddle-limbed marine reptile

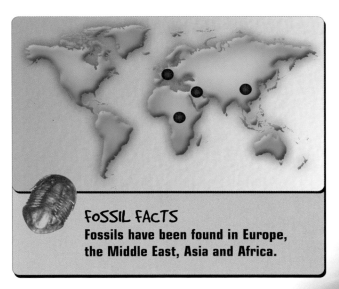

FOSSIL FACTS
Fossils have been found in Europe, the Middle East, Asia and Africa.

interlocking teeth acted like a trap for fish — once it got a grip, Nothosaurus did not easily let go.

Powerful legs and a strong tail made Nothosaurus a very strong swimmer. Although it certainly hunted its food in the water, Nothosaurus probably did not live in the water all the

Nothosaurus means 'false lizard'. It was not a dinosaur at all, in spite of its lizard-like appearance. It is one of a whole group of reptiles called **nothosaurs**. This group was named by G. von Meunster in 1834.

Nothosaurs

Nothosaurs were long-tailed and long-necked fish-eating marine reptiles. They covered an incredible range of sizes, from less than 20 cm (8 in.) to 6 m (20 ft) long! All of them had four broad, paddle-shaped limbs, probably with webbed fingers and toes. They had long necks, a narrow head with long, thin snouts and nostrils on top so they could breathe while swimming. They may have also had a fin on their tails to help them steer in the water.

It is difficult to give a 'typical' size for this marine reptile, since we know of at least eight different species of Nothosaurus. Between 1 and 3 m (3 and 10 ft) is probably correct.

In its mouth were fang-like teeth that pointed outwards, suggesting its main diet was fish. Smaller teeth lined its jaws all the way to the back of its cheeks. Its sharp,

Dinosaur Data

PRONUNCIATION:	NO-THO-**SAWR**-US
SUBORDER:	NOTHOSAURIA
FAMILY:	NOTHOSAURIDAE
DESCRIPTION:	FISH-EATING MARINE REPTILE
FEATURES:	PADDLE-LIKE LIMBS, LONG POINTED TAIL
DIET:	FISH AND SHRIMP

time like its descendants the later **plesiosaurs**. It would have come up onto rocks and beaches, just like a seal, to rest. Scientists believe it also came up on land to lay its eggs. Many fossils of young Nothosaurus have been discovered in what were caves during the Triassic period. Few creatures at that time lived in caves, making them a safe place for the eggs.

MEGA FACTS

- Scientists have found at least eight different kinds of Nothosaur.

- Nothosaurs went extinct during the late Triassic period. They may have evolved into the plesiosaurs.

- Primitive dinosaurs like Lesothosaurus (see page 167) and Herrerasaurus (see page 90) were just beginning to appear on earth at the time Nothosaurus lived.

LIOPLEURODON

Sea-living reptile

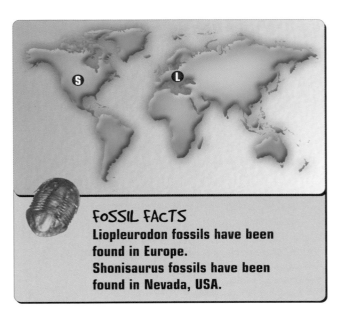

FOSSIL FACTS
Liopleurodon fossils have been found in Europe.
Shonisaurus fossils have been found in Nevada, USA.

Liopleurodon was a type of pliosaur, or short-necked **plesiosaur** (the short-necked forms are known as pliosaurs). Plesiosaurs were actually a type of reptile that had returned to the sea. They were around in the early Jurassic period and were split into two groups: long-necked and short-necked.

Liopleurodon had huge flippers that propelled it through the water. It would have quietly cruised through the shallow sea looking for its next unsuspecting meal!

As it was a successful hunter, Liopleurodon would have had a set of long jaws and needle-sharp teeth. It probably would have preyed on marine crocodiles, the giant fish Leedsichthys, Ichthyosaurus and possibly other pliosaurs.

Liopleurodon actually breathed air, but it never left the sea. Because of this it would have given birth to live young, and probably swam into shallower waters to breed.

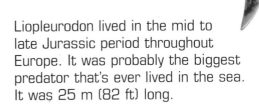

Liopleurodon lived in the mid to late Jurassic period throughout Europe. It was probably the biggest predator that's ever lived in the sea. It was 25 m (82 ft) long.

Dinosaur Data

PRONUNCIATION:	**LIE**-OH-**PLOO**-RO-DON
SUBORDER:	PLIOSAUROIDEA
FAMILY:	PLIOSAUR
DESCRIPTION:	ENORMOUS AQUATIC **OMNIVORE**
FEATURES:	DOMINANT PREDATOR
DIET:	MARINE CROCODILES, LEEDSICHTHYS, ICHTHYOSAURUS, POSSIBLY OTHER PLIOSAURS

SHONISAURUS

Sea-living reptile

Dinosaur Data

PRONUNCIATION:	SHON-E-SAWR-US
SUBORDER:	LONGIPINNATI
FAMILY:	SHASTASAURIDAE
DESCRIPTION:	DOLPHIN-LIKE SEA CREATURE
FEATURES:	PREDATORY REPTILE
DIET:	FISH

Shonisaurus was a type of reptile that lived during the time of the dinosaurs in North America. Large numbers of their bones were discovered in a small area in Berlin, Nevada, USA.

Shonisaurus was an ichthyosaur that lived during the late Triassic period, and looked very much like a dolphin. However, its body was a huge 15 m (49 ft) long so it was more like a whale in size.

Shonisaurus also had four fin-like flippers instead of two, a dorsal fin and a fish-like tail. It had long thin jaws, with sharp needle-like teeth that were only at the front. It used these jaws to catch fish. They probably also ate ammonites. There would have been plenty of these in the sea at this time.

MEGA FACTS

- Fossils have been found of the remains of the victims of Liopleurodon. Teeth marks in other plesiosaur flippers and remains of other creatures show just how ferocious the Liopleurodon were.

- Liopleurodon had nostrils in its skull, which allowed it to smell its prey in the water.

- In 2003 it is thought that a fossil pliosaur, that could have been a Liopleurodon, was discovered in Mexico, which measured 18 m (59 ft) long. It was still young, so it could have grown much larger than this.

- Miners discovered the first bones of the Shonisaurus and it is thought that they used its backbone segments as dinner plates.

51

ATTACK AND DEFENCE

Dinosaurs attacked each other, defended themselves and competed for leadership within groups. Even though some of the dinosaurs could be deadly, most of them were peaceful **herbivores** that never attacked. Herbivore dinosaurs usually tried to escape before fighting. Their means of attack and defence were either used to defend themselves or to compete for food, space and a mate within their group.

Defence

Dinosaurs defended themselves by disguise, herding together, or fighting back. Some of the small plant eaters found that running away was often the best way to stay alive! Good hearing and eyesight was essential for fast running at the first sign of danger.

Means of attack and defence ranged from the active use of teeth, claws and horns to passive means like camouflage and armour.

Many plant eaters protected vulnerable body parts, such as necks and spines, with bony neck frills, tooth-snapping bone studs and plates and many had a sharp claw, horn or spike for swift counter-attack.

Some dinosaurs were large enough for their size alone to be a defence. There were no other predators big enough to tackle an adult.

Dinosaurs that lived in herds for protection competed with each other for social order, for example to see who would be the leader. The fighting didn't usually end in death or serious injury though, because the dinosaurs didn't want to reduce the size of the herd.

Attack

Dinosaurs which were **carnivores** had ferocious weapons which could kill other dinosaurs, such as sharp teeth or powerful legs for speed and leaping attacks.

Acrocanthosaurus

Daspletosaurus used its powerful jaw armed with a large number of sharp, strong teeth. Deinonychus (see page 58) was very agile and used its front and hind claws to hang onto and injure other dinosaurs.

Scelidosaurus

Therizinosaurus had giant claws, which it would wave at an enemy to show the size of them. Troodon (see page 82), a small flat-footed predator, had 3-D vision eyes which probably allowed it to stalk small mammals that came out at dusk, when others could not see in the dark.

Therizinosaurus

Allosaurus (see page 72), when hunting alone, would have attacked small to medium-sized dinosaurs, but when pack-hunting several Allosaurus would have been capable of bringing down very large dinosaurs such as Diplodocus (see page 98).

The terrifying Postosuchus was a hunter who could attack and kill almost any animal of its time. It hunted other large animals by a combination of stealth and ambush so that it could take its prey by surprise.

Compsognathus

TYRANNOSAURUS REX

King of the tyrant lizards

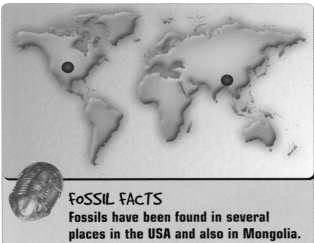

FOSSIL FACTS
Fossils have been found in several places in the USA and also in Mongolia.

Powerful hind legs and very large feet would have enabled Tyrannosaurus Rex to walk and, probably even run for long distances in search of food. Even though its hands were tiny, they were armed with savage claws for ripping and tearing flesh from its prey. Its sharp teeth allowed it to rip flesh from a carcass and it could crush and grind the bones with its powerful jaw. It was also an opportunistic feeder and would also scavenge for dead animals whenever fresh food was in short supply.

Tyrannosaurus Rex was one of the biggest and most powerful dinosaurs. It was first discovered in 1902 and was named in 1905.

Tyrannosaurus Rex probably lived in family groups. Smaller dinosaurs would have been subjected its fierce and often fatal attacks. Large Tyrannosaurus Rex bite marks have been identified in the fossils of other dinosaurs.

Dinosaur Data

PRONUNCIATION:	TIE-RAN-O-SAW-RUS REX
SUBORDER:	THERAPODA
FAMILY:	TYRANNOSAUROIDEA
DESCRIPTION:	LARGE, POWERFUL CARNIVORE
FEATURES:	DOMINANT PREDATOR
DIET:	HUNTED AND SCAVENGED

Permian period	Triassic period	Jurassic period	Cretaceous period
(290-248 million years ago)	(248-176 million years ago)	(176-130 million years ago)	(130-65 million years ago)

Appearance

Tyrannosaurus Rex was 4.5–6 m (15–20 ft) tall and would have been able to see through the tops of the trees in the swampy forest it lived in.

The most recently discovered Tyrannosaurus Rex fossil was found in South Dakota in 1990; she's been called Sue after the woman who found her and is now on display in the Field Museum in Chicago.

MEGA FACTS

- Over 12 m (39 ft) long from the nose to the end of tail.

- Could move at 16–48 km/h (10–30 mph).

- Powerful jaw of 58 serrated teeth each 15 cm (6 in.) long which re-grew when they were damaged.

- 200 bones in a full Tyrannosaurus skeleton — roughly the same number as a human.

- Fossil Sue was auctioned at Sotheby's for $7.6 million in 1997.

Dinosaur experts continue to search for new fossils and examine those already found to learn more about how this giant **carnivore** lived and died.

GIGANOTOSAURUS

Giant southern lizard (new king of the carnivores)

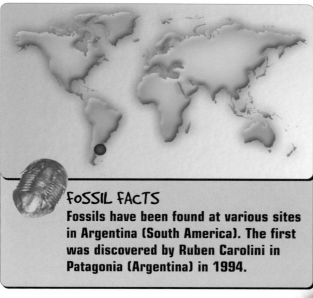

FOSSIL FACTS
Fossils have been found at various sites in Argentina (South America). The first was discovered by Ruben Carolini in Patagonia (Argentina) in 1994.

side to side. It would also have helped Giganotosaurus make quick turns. From its skull, we know that it probably had a good sense of smell and excellent eyesight thanks to its large eyes.

Giganotosaurus walked on two legs, had a long slim tail, and had enormous jaws in its 1.8 m (6 ft) skull.

Attacking prey

Those jaws were lined with serrated teeth, well adapted for slicing into flesh and up to 20 cm (8 in.) long.

Giganotosaurus means 'Giant Southern Lizard'. It was given its name in 1995 by Coria and Salgado.

Giganotosaurus lived at the same time as enormous plant-eating dinosaurs like Argentinosaurus (see page 96) which it could hunt and eat. Like Tyrannosaurus Rex (see page 54), which lived 30 million years later, it hunted in warm, swampy areas.

Appearance

Giganotosaurus was 5.5 m (18 ft) high and measured up to 15 m (49 ft) long but is not the largest dinosaur of all time; Argentinosaurus is the largest dinosaur at the moment and there may be more that we have not discovered yet. In 2006, scientists suggested that Gigantosaurus now been displaced as largest **carnivore** by Spinosaurus (see page 78), based on a study of new finds.

Although larger than T-Rex, Giganotosaurus was more lightly built, and it is thought it could run quite fast. Its slender, pointed tail would have helped to balance it out as it ran, probably moving from

Permian period	Triassic period	Jurassic period	Cretaceous period
(290-248 million years ago)	(248-176 million years ago)	(176-130 million years ago)	(130-66 million years ago)

It did not have the powerful crushing bite of T-Rex, and so would have attacked by slashing. It had three clawed fingers it could use to slash, or grasp with.

When hunting, it would probably have singled out dinosaurs that were young, or weak, or separated from the herd. Fossil evidence where several skeletons were found close together suggests that they may have hunted and lived in packs.

Giganotosaurs may have cooperated in tasks like hunting and protecting their young.

MEGA FACTS

- Weighed as much as 125 people.

- Appeared in 3-D in the IMAX® film *Dinosaurs*. Also in the *Walking with dinosaurs* special *Land of giants*, in which a pack of Giganotosaurs bring down an Argentinosaurus.

- The biggest Giganotosaurus was over a metre longer and a ton heavier than 'Sue', the largest known Tyrannosaurus Rex.

- May have hunted prey up to ten times its own size.

- Giganotosaurus had a skull the size of a bathtub, but its brain was only the size (and shape) of a banana.

Note This is not the same dinosaur as the African sauropod Gigantosaurus (different spelling) named by Seeley in 1869.

Dinosaur Data

PRONUNCIATION:	JIG-A-**NOT**-OH-**SAWR**-US
SUBORDER:	THERAPODA
FAMILY:	ALLOSAURIDAE
DESCRIPTION:	LARGE POWERFUL CARNIVORE
FEATURES:	DOMINANT PREDATOR

DEINONYCHUS

Cunning bipedal hunter

FOSSIL FACTS
The first fossils were found in 1964 by Grant E. Meyer and John H. Ostrom in southern Montana.

The name Deinonychus means 'terrible claw' and comes from the Greek words *deinos* (terrible) and *onychus* (claw). The name was given by John Ostrom in 1969 because of the long, wickedly sharp claw found on the second toe of each of its feet.

Appearance

This carnivorous dinosaur was **bipedal**. It was about 1.5 m (4 ft) tall, weighed about 80 kg (176 lb) and measured 3 m (10 ft) from the tip of its nose to the end of its long, rigid tail. It had a large head with powerful jaws and sharp serrated teeth. Large eye sockets indicate it probably also had excellent eyesight.

Permian period	Triassic period	Jurassic period	Cretaceous period
(290-240 million years ago)	(248-178 million years ago)	(176-130 million years ago)	(130-65 million years ago)

MEGA FACTS

- Fossil evidence shows Deinonychus packs hunted and killed Tenontosaurus, a dinosaur ten times their size.

- There is some evidence that Deinonychus may have had feathers.

Its feet were four-toed and it was the second toe that sported the vicious 13 cm (5 in.) long claw after which it was named. This claw could be held up out of the way whilst the creature was running, only snapping into position when needed for the attack. Deinonychus also had a pair of arms that ended in three-fingered hands with each finger having a curved claw that was long and sharp.

The long claw

Initially, it was thought that the long claw on its second toe was used to slash prey but recent tests have shown that it was actually more likely used as a stabbing weapon. Deinonychus' likely method of attack was to use its powerful back legs to leap into the air and land on its prey, kicking the long sickle toe-claws in, causing significant damage and anchoring it firmly. It would then tear and bite at the prey to cause as much blood loss as possible.

Its long tail was stiffened with bony rods along the spine. This tail would have acted like a counterweight, giving Deinonychus excellent balance and allowing it to make very fast turns as it chased down prey. We also strongly believe that Deinonychus hunted in packs, as several fossils of groups of Deinonychus have been found. Hunting in packs would have allowed Deinonychus to take on prey that would be too large for a single Deinonychus.

Brain size

The dromaeosauridae family all have quite large brains in comparison to their total body size, indicating that they were probably much more intelligent than other dinosaurs. This would have allowed them to work together as a team during the hunt and use simple tactics to guide their prey towards other members of the pack.

Deinonychus

Dinosaur Data

PRONUNCIATION:	DYN-**ON**-IK-US
SUBORDER:	THEROPODA
FAMILY:	DROMAEOSAURIDAE
DESCRIPTION:	FAST, AGILE BIPEDAL PREDATOR
FEATURES:	SICKLE CLAW ON EACH FOOT, LARGE BRAINS, LONG RIGID TAIL
DIET:	CARNIVOROUS

Fish-eating dinosaur

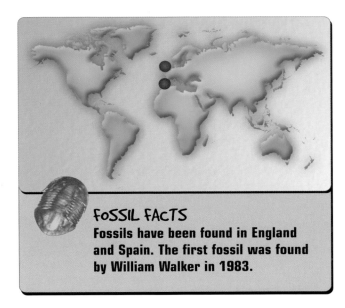

FOSSIL FACTS
Fossils have been found in England and Spain. The first fossil was found by William Walker in 1983.

shaped necks of other **therapods**) that supported a skull with a long jaw and many teeth, a long tail (which helped it to balance), two long back legs and two slightly shorter front legs, each of which had a 30 cm (12 in.) long curved claw.

The size and shape of Baryonyx's back legs suggest it would have been a fast runner as the thigh bone is relatively short compared to the calf. Baryonyx's neck would have been angled slightly downwards.

Teeth and diet

Baryonyx's teeth were very unusual for dinosaurs – the cutting edges were much finer.

Baryonyx means 'heavy claw' and comes from the Greek words *bary* (heavy) and *onyx* (claw). It was named by Angela C. Milner and Alan J. Charig in 1987, because of the 30 cm (12 in.) long curved claw found on each of the creature's hands. So far only two Baryonyx fossils have been found.

Appearance

Even though only two fossils have been found it has still been possible to learn a lot about this dinosaur because the first find was so complete. Baryonyx was about 9.5 m (31 ft) long, 5 m (16 ft) tall and probably weighed about 2,500 kg (2.5 tons). It had a long straight neck (unlike the 'S'

| Permian period (290-248 million years ago) | Triassic period (248-176 million years ago) | Jurassic period (176-130 million years ago) | Cretaceous period (130-66 million years ago) |

This would have meant they were not well suited to tearing meat but would instead have been very good at holding prey in place. This suggested that Baryonyx was ideally suited for eating fish. Fossils of scales from a 1 m (3 ft) long fish called Lepidotes have been found in the stomach area of a Baronyx fossil. Scientists believe that Baryonyx would have waited on the banks or in shallow waters for fish to move past and may have used its large claws to scoop them out of the water. It could also have held its head underwater and snapped fish up directly as its nostrils were high enough up on its skull for it to have its jaws underwater and still be able to breathe.

MEGA FACTS

- Baryonyx type name is Baryonyx Walkeri – named after the amateur fossil hunter William Walker who found the first fossil.

- Baryonyx's upper jaw had a sharp angle near the snout, a feature seen in crocodiles that helps to prevent prey from escaping.

- Baryonyx was the first meat-eating dinosaur to be discovered in England and the first fish-eating dinosaur to be discovered anywhere.

Dinosaur Data

PRONUNCIATION:	BAR-EE-ON-IKS
SUBORDER:	THERAPODA
FAMILY:	SPINOSAURIDAE
DESCRIPTION:	LOW-SLUNG FISH-EATING DINOSAUR
FEATURES:	LONG STRAIGHT NECK, 96 SHARP TEETH WITH MICROSCOPIC SERRATIONS, 30 CM CLAWS ON ITS HANDS.
DIET:	FISH; BARYONYX WAS A PISCIVORE AND WAS THE FIRST OF ONLY TWO FISH-EATING DINOSAURS TO BE DISCOVERED SO FAR (THE OTHER IS SUCHOMIMUS)

COMPSOGNATHUS

Tiny, fleet-footed predator

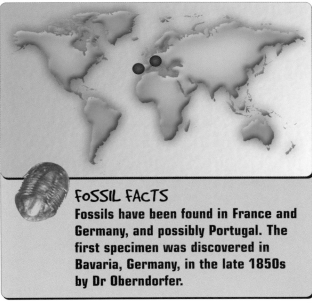

FOSSIL FACTS
Fossils have been found in France and Germany, and possibly Portugal. The first specimen was discovered in Bavaria, Germany, in the late 1850s by Dr Oberndorfer.

that Compsognathus was capable of rapid acceleration, high speed, flexibility, and quick reactions.

We know its size from two almost complete skeletons. Study of other partial skeletons gives a range of size from 70–140 cm (28–56 in.). It weighed only around 3.6 kg (8 lb) when fully-grown, and stood not much more than half a metre (1ft 6 in.) tall.

Palaeontologists cannot agree over whether Compsognathus had two or three fingers on each hand. Either way, those slender fingers would have helped

Compsognathus means 'elegant jaw' and comes from the Greek words *kompos* (elegant) and *gnathos* (jaw). It was named for the delicate bones of its lightly-built skull. It was given this name in 1859, by Johann A. Wagner.

Compsognathus was an early member of a group of dinosaurs called the **coelurosaurs** ('hollow-tail lizards'). Later members of the coelurosaur group included the most likely ancestors of birds. Compsognathus had hollow bones throughout its body. This made it very light and fast.

Appearance

Compsognathus ran on its long, thin hind legs and had surprisingly short arms. It had a long tail to act as a counterbalance and to stabilise it during fast turns. Its head was small and pointed and it had a long, flexible neck. Its skull suggests it had good eyesight and was probably pretty intelligent. The characteristics of its skull and legs tell us

Permian period	Triassic period	Jurassic period	Cretaceous period
(290-248 million years ago)	(248-176 million years ago)	(176-130 million years ago)	(130 million years ago)

with grasping prey, which could then be swallowed whole or torn into pieces by tiny, sharp teeth.

Habitat

At the time Compsognathus lived, water covered much of what is now France and southern Germany. Compsognathus lived on islands in this sea. Although very small, it was probably the largest predator where it lived – the small islands did not have enough vegetation to support large **herbivores**, which in turn meant there was no tempting prey for large **carnivores**.

MEGA FACTS

- Compsognathus appeared in *Jurassic Park II* and *Jurassic Park III* as the vicious 'compys'. These films showed them hunting in packs, but in fact we have no idea whether they did this or not.

- Even fully grown, Compsognathus would weigh no more than a turkey.

- According to calculations made using the distance between fossilised footprints, Compsognathus could run at speeds up to 40 km/h (25 mph).

- The first fossil skeleton of this dinosaur that was found had the remains of a fast-running lizard called bavarisaurus in its stomach.

- In recent years the remains of even smaller dinosaurs have been found. These included the 50 cm (18 in.) long plant-eating Micropachycephalosaurus, which as well as being the smallest dinosaur in the world also has the longest name!

- Evidence of feathers has yet to be discovered on a Compsognathus fossil.

Dinosaur Data

PRONUNCIATION:	KOMP-SOG-**NAY**-THUS *OR* KOMP-SO-**NATH**-US
SUBORDER:	THEROPODA
FAMILY:	COMPSOGNATHIDAE
DESCRIPTION:	BIPEDAL CARNIVORE
FEATURES:	HOLLOW BONES
DIET:	SMALL ANIMALS

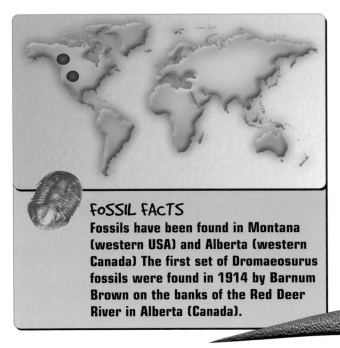

FOSSIL FACTS
Fossils have been found in Montana (western USA) and Alberta (western Canada) The first set of Dromaeosurus fossils were found in 1914 by Barnum Brown on the banks of the Red Deer River in Alberta (Canada).

It had a large head, containing a big brain – scientists believe it was one of the most intelligent of the dinosaurs. It also had excellent vision thanks to its large eyes, and probably a strong sense of smell and good hearing, making it an efficient hunter. Its jaws were long and strong, and contained long, razor-sharp teeth.

Attack

Dromaeosaurus' most dangerous weapons were its claws, which were sickle-shaped and on the end of each finger. Prey was probably gripped with the claws of the foot, while the

Dromaeosaurus means 'fast-running lizard'. It was given this name in 1922 by Barnum Brown and William Matthew. It is part of a group of dinosaurs known as **dromaeosaurs**, which are the dinosaurs believed to be most closely related to modern day birds.

When first discovered, Dromaeosaurus was hard to classify. It wasn't until nearly 50 years after its discovery that Dromaeosaurus was formally classified into its own family.

Appearance

Dromaeosaurus was active and agile. It was about the size of a large dog, and balanced itself while running (and even standing on one leg so as to slash at prey with its clawed toes) with the help of its long, stiff tail.

The tail was stiffened by a lattice of bony rods and was flexible at the base so that it could be moved up and down.

Fossil of a juvenile Sinonithosaurus

Skeleton of a Dromaeosaurus

MEGA FACTS

- Dromaeosaurus teeth have been found among the fossils of much larger dinosaurs, leading some scientists to suggest that they hunted in packs like wolves, so that they could bring down larger prey.

- With its deep, large jaw, short and massive skull, and big strong teeth, Dromaeosaurus closely resembles the much larger Tyrannosaurs.

- In 2001, a remarkable fossilised skeleton was loaned from China to the American Museum of Natural History. Scientists believe it to be that of a Dromaeosaurus – with feathers from head to foot!

- It ate small and medium-sized plant eaters like young Triceratops and baby duckbills.

- All 'raptors' (as dromaeosaurs came to be nicknamed) have the sickle-shaped killing claw on the hind feet – this was used for disembowelling prey.

finger claws slashed at the victim, though the sharp, hooked claw on each leg could certainly do some horrendous damage of its own. Dromaeosaurus probably hunted by running and leaping at its prey, enabling it to use all four limbs in the attack as it launched itself at the target.

Dinosaur Data

PRONUNCIATION:	**DROH**-MEE-OH-**SAWR**-US
SUBORDER:	THEROPODA
FAMILY:	DROMAEOSAURIDAE
DESCRIPTION:	ACTIVE, AGILE BIPEDAL HUNTER
FEATURES:	MASSIVE SLASHING CLAWS
DIET:	CARNIVORE, POSSIBLE SCAVENGER

VELOCIRAPTOR

Swift and vicious bipedal carnivore

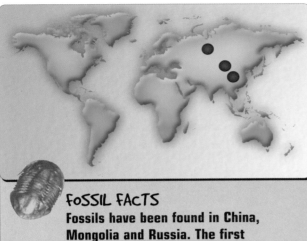

FOSSIL FACTS
Fossils have been found in China, Mongolia and Russia. The first Velociraptor fossils were found in 1914.

around 80 sharp bladed teeth – some of the teeth were over 2.5 cm (1 in.) long. It possessed large eyes, which gave it excellent vision even in the dark.

Velociraptor had an enlarged second toe with a vicious oversized claw attached to it. These sickle-like claws could be raised off the ground while running or walking, then used once the Velociraptor launched an attack.

Velociraptor means 'speedy thief'. This carnivore lived in a desert-like environment around 70 million years ago, and may have hunted in packs, preying largely on **herbivores** like Hadrosaurus (see page 104).

Appearance

It was about 1.5–2 m (5–6 ft), and stood on two legs. It had long arms and a long straight tail. Its strong jaws contained

Dinosaur Data

PRONUNCIATION:	VUH-**LOSS**-IH-**RAP**-TOR
SUBORDER:	THERAPODA
FAMILY:	DROMAESORIDAE
DESCRIPTION:	SMALL, SWIFT CARNIVORE
FEATURES:	VERY INTELLIGENT, BIPEDAL
DIET:	HUNTED AND POSSIBLY SCAVENGED

| Permian period (290-248 million years ago) | Triassic period (248-176 million years ago) | Jurassic period (176-130 million years ago) | Cretaceous period (130-65 million years ago) |

The claw experiments

In 2005 Dr Phil Manning performed experiments using a robotic claw designed to mimic the attack of a Velociraptor. The results showed that, against larger prey with tough skin, the claw would not have made wounds deep enough to kill quickly. The large claws were probably used to pierce and hold prey. Its razor-sharp teeth would then tear into the prey, causing as much blood loss as possible to vulnerable areas.

MEGA FACTS

- Recent scientific thinking is that Velociraptor was very close to being birdlike, and may well have been covered in primitive feathers for warmth and display.

- Scientists believe a Velociraptor could leap up to 3.6 m (12 ft) to attack its prey.

- Velociraptor could run up to about 60 km/h (37 mph).

- They were probably warm-blooded in some degree.

- The Velociraptor had a very big brain compared to its body size, making it one of the most intelligent of the dinosaurs.

Breathing

Some scientists now believe raptors could have had a way of breathing like modern birds. Birds store extra air in air sacs inside their hollow bones as well as using their lungs – this means they can extract oxygen from air much more efficiently than mammals. A comparison between bird anatomy and fossilised dinosaur remains revealed many similarities.

Fossilised attack

An especially interesting fossil was discovered in 1971 in the Gobi Desert – it revealed a Velociraptor in mid-attack on a Protoceratops (see page 138). The claws of the Velociraptor were buried in the body of the Protoceratops, its sickle claws close to where the jugular vein would have been – but the Protoceratops has the raptor's arm firmly in its jaws. Both seem to have died in a sudden sandstorm, or landslip, preserving their battle forever.

OVIRAPTOR PHILOCARATOPS

Odd-looking omnivorous raptor

FOSSIL FACTS
Fossils have been found in Mongolia. The first fossils were found in the Gobi Desert in 1924.

Oviraptor was a small, fast-moving **biped** with long slender legs and short arms for grasping. At the ends of these arms were large three-fingered hands with claws up to 8 cm (3 in.) long. It had a flexible neck, a long tail, its powerful jaws were designed for crushing and its skull was almost parrot-shaped. On top of its snout was a thin bony crest, which seemed to change with age.

The shape of Oviraptor's head and mouth would have made it equipped for dealing with a variety of food. It was probably an **omnivore**, making up its diet from almost anything it could find – for example, meat, plants, eggs, insects and shellfish. Omnivorous dinosaurs are very rare.

Oviraptor philoceratops means 'egg thief, fond of horned dinosaurs'.

Permian period	Triassic period	Jurassic period	Cretaceous period
(290-248 million years ago)	(248-176 million years ago)	(176-130 million years ago)	(130-65 million years ago)

Fossil

Wrongly accused

The original fossil find was misinterpreted by the scientists that studied it. They found the fossil of the Oviraptor near a nest containing dinosaur eggs – these eggs were assumed to belong to another dinosaur. The scientists thought the Ovirapor must have been stealing the eggs for food and so gave it its name of 'egg thief'.

In 1993 a team of American and Mongolian scientists found a fossil of an egg of the same kind – and this time found an Oviraptor embryo inside it. It seemed that the Oviraptor found in 1924 had been protecting its own nest!

Further evidence of the Oviraptor's 'nurturing' nature came with the discovery in 1995 of a fossil Oviraptor actually sitting on its nest. The Oviraptor had its feet folded underneath its body, and a clutch of at least 15 eggs were arranged in a circle and surrounded by its forearms.

Reproduction

A recent discovery from Jiangxi in China showed a partial skeleton of an Oviraptor who was about to give birth, with intact eggs with shells still inside the body. Examination of the find showed that the reproductive system of an Oviraptor is something between that of reptiles and birds, having similarities to each. This is taken as further evidence of the theory that birds evolved from dinosaurs.

MEGA FACTS

- Oviraptor could run at about 70 km/h (43 mph).

- It was 1.8–2.5 m (6–8 ft) long and weighed about 36 kg (80 lb).

- If an Oviraptor sat on its eggs to keep them warm, that would mean it was warm-blooded. However, they may have sat on their eggs for other reasons, like protecting them.

- Its crest may have been used for mating display, or to distinguish between males and females.

- Oviraptors share many characteristics with birds, and may have been covered in feathers.

Dinosaur Data

PRONUNCIATION:	O-VIH-**RAP**-TOR
SUBORDER:	THERAPODA
FAMILY:	OVIRAPTORIDAE
DESCRIPTION:	BIPEDAL OMNIVORE
FEATURES:	TOOTHLESS BEAK, HORNY CREST IN TOP OF HEAD
DIET:	OMNIVOROUS

ACROCANTHOSAURUS

Gigantic bipedal hunter

Acrocanthosaurus means 'high-spined lizard'. It gets this name from the unusual spikes which grew out of its spine.

Appearance

'Acro' (as the dinosaur is often nicknamed) was 13 m (42 ft) in length and weighed 2300 kg (5,000 lb). Acro's teeth were designed for tearing meat from the bones of its prey, not for crushing and cracking.

Acro was a meat eater, and had a skull very similar to that of Allosaurus (see page 72). It had typical Allosaur 'eye horns', developed into ridges to protect the eyes – a second ridge ran along the top of the nose and joined up with the eye ridges. The unusually deep back part of its lower jaw gave it a very powerful bite. Its hands were nothing like an Allosaur's, however – it had three-fingered hands equipped with sickle-shaped claws, shaped for holding prey rather than puncturing skin.

The spines

The tall spines on the backbone of Acrocanthosaurus ran from its neck down to the front half of its

FOSSIL FACTS
Fossils have been found in Oklahoma, Texas, Utah and Arizona, all in the USA. The first specimens were found in the early 1950s, and a complete skeleton was discovered in Atoka County (Oklahoma) in 1983 by Cephis Hall and Sid Love.

| Permian period (290-248 million years ago) | Triassic period (248-176 million years ago) | Jurassic period (176-130 million years ago) | Cretaceous period (130-66 million years ago) |

tail. Scientists originally thought this must mean it had a 'sail' on its back like Dimetrodon (see page 16). More recent thinking is that had more of a 'hump-backed' shape than a sail, but the exact purpose of the spines is still a mystery.

They may have been anchors for powerful muscles. If so, it would mean Acro was very strong indeed — and it would have needed to be to catch the huge **sauropod** dinosaurs its fossilised footprints show it tracking! Some modern animals, for example, elephants, horses and buffalo, have this kind of muscle suspension.

The spines might also have been used to communicate with other Acros, and to regulate body temperature. They would have provided Acro with extra surface area, which would be helpful for both the display of colour and pattern, and for absorbing and getting rid of heat. This would have been very useful in the tropical climate in which it lived.

Dinosaur Data

PRONUNCIATION:	AK-ROW-**KAN** THO-**SAWR**-US
SUBORDER:	THERAPODA
DESCRIPTION:	LARGE, POWERFUL MEAT EATER
FEATURES:	TALL RIDGE SPINES
DIET:	CARNIVORE AND POSSIBLY SCAVENGER

MEGA FACTS

- This dinosaur would probably be able to lift a small car off the ground if it were alive today. Its arms were larger and more powerful than those of T-Rex itself.

- Acrocanthosaurus appeared in the multi-platform video game *Jurassic Park: Operation Genesis.* It is shown catching a Dryosaurus for dinner.

- In 2005, scientists constructed a replica of Acro's brain, using CT scanning technology on a fossil skull. The result showed that the brain was more like that of a crocodile than a bird in shape, that Acro probably had excellent hearing, and that its head would have been held at an angle 25 degrees beneath horizontal.

- As any of its 68 serrated teeth broke, another was ready to take its place. Like a shark, Acro was constantly shedding old teeth and replacing them with new ones.

- In 1998, the fossil skeleton of an Acrocanthosaurus nicknamed 'Fran' was bought for the North Carolina Museum of Natural Sciences for $3 million, believed to be the second highest price ever paid for a dinosaur.

ALLOSAURUS

Dominant flesh eater

very powerful arms. It also had large claws on its hands – one claw discovered was more than 350 cm (11 ft) long.

Allosaurus was light thanks to air sacs in its bones – this would have allowed it to run very fast, and also to leap at its prey, tear out a chunk with its teeth and then leap away again.

FOSSIL FACTS
Fossils have been found in the Western USA and (recently) in Europe. The first fossils were found in Colarado, USA.

Allosaurus means 'different lizard', so named because its vertebrae (backbones) were different from those of all other dinosaurs. The first specimen was studied and named by Othniel C. March in 1877.

Appearance

Allosaurus was between 7–12 m (23–39 ft) in length, 3–4.5 m (10–15 ft) tall and weighed 1,000–4,500 kg (1–4 tons). It had a huge head, long strong hind legs and

Dinosaur Data

PRONUNCIATION:	AL-UH-**SAWR**-US
SUBORDER:	THERAPODA
FAMILY:	ALLOSAURIDAE
DESCRIPTION:	BIPEDAL CARNIVORE
FEATURES:	HINGED JAW, BLUNT HORNS
DIET:	PLANT-EATING DINOSAURS

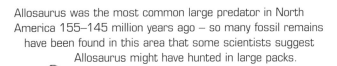

Allosaurus was the most common large predator in North America 155–145 million years ago – so many fossil remains have been found in this area that some scientists suggest Allosaurus might have hunted in large packs.

Skeletons

In 1991, a 95% complete skeleton of a young Allosaurus was discovered and named 'Big Al'. Big Al was 8 m (26 ft) in length and 19 of his bones showed signs of breakage or infection. He was discovered by a Swiss team led by Kirby Siber. The same team later excavated an even more impressive Allosaurus skeleton – the best preserved of its kind to date – which was promptly christened 'Big Al 2'.

Attacking prey

Recently, more information has come to light about the way an Allosaurus attacked its prey. A scientist at Cambridge University (England) called Emily Rayfield created a computer model of Big Al's skull, using techniques usually used in engineering.

The model allowed her to calculate the force that Big Al's jaws would have needed to break the skull of a living creature. She concluded that Allosaurus actually had quite a weak bite.

The skull was also very light, but capable of withstanding massive upwards force. Rayfield concluded that the Allosaur had actually attacked by opening its mouth wide and using powerful neck muscles to drive its upper jaw downward, slamming into its prey like an axe and tearing away hunks of flesh.

MEGA FACTS

- Allosaurus jaws were able to 'expand' to allow larger chunks of food to be swallowed.

- Allosaurus has featured in several films.

- Footprint evidence suggests that Allosaurus hunted in packs, and may have raised its young in large nests.

- An Allosaurus could run at almost 60 km/h (37 mph).

SAURORNITHOIDES

Big-brained bird-like carnivore

Saurornithoides means 'bird-like lizard'. It was named in 1924 by Osborn and comes from the Greek stems *saur* (lizard) *ornitho* (bird) and *oid* (form).

Like other members of its family, Saurornithoides was a highly-efficient predator. It had a long, low head and sharp, closely-packed teeth. Like other raptors, it ran on its strong hind legs and probably used its long arms and grasping hands to seize and tear at live prey, including small mammals and possibly other dinosaur hatchlings.

It had one especially long, vicious claw on its hind feet, which was attached to the fourth toe, and was retractable when running or walking.

Much of what we know about this dinosaur comes from fossilised skull material – no complete skeleton has been found anywhere.

Dinosaur Data

PRONUNCIATION:	**SAWR**-OR-NIH-**THOY**-DEEZ
SUBORDER:	THERAPODA
FAMILY:	TROODONTIDAE
DESCRIPTION:	BIRD-LIKE BIPEDAL CARNIVORE
FEATURES:	HUGE RETRACTABLE CLAW, BIG BRAIN
DIET:	SMALLER MAMMALS, INSECTS

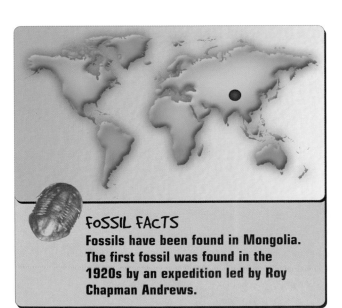

FOSSIL FACTS
Fossils have been found in Mongolia. The first fossil was found in the 1920s by an expedition led by Roy Chapman Andrews.

Permian period (290-248 million years ago)	Triassic period (248-176 million years ago)	Jurassic period (176-130 million years ago)	Cretaceous period (130-65 million years ago)

Skulls

The skull fossils show that Saurornithoides had a very large brain compared to the size of its body, making it one of the most intelligent of the dinosaurs. Its brain was six times as big as that of a crocodile.

The skulls also show that this dinosaur had large eyes, positioned forward so as to give it **binocular vision**. This would have been a big help while hunting – for example, allowing Saurornithoides to accurately judge distances. Most dinosaurs had eyes on the sides of their heads. It probably also had excellent night vision, and may even have been primarily nocturnal.

When the first Saurornithoides fossils were discovered, its long, narrow snout tricked those studying it into thinking it was actually an ancient bird. There is still debate as to just how like a bird the 'lizard bird form' really was. Many scientists, for example, now believe its body may have been covered in feathers. Further study (and, hopefully, new discoveries) will be needed before the secrets of this smart little dinosaur are revealed.

MEGA FACTS

- Estimated to be 2–3 m (6–10 ft) in length.

- Weighed about 13–27 kg (29–59 lb).

- Fossils from very similar dinosaurs have been found in North America, suggesting that 85–77 million years ago, the climates of Mongolia and North America were similar.

- It was a smart dinosaur as it had the biggest brain relative to its body size of any of the dinosaurs.

- It was also sharp-eyed as it had large eyes and binocular vision.

75

CARNOTAURUS

Horned gigantic carnivore

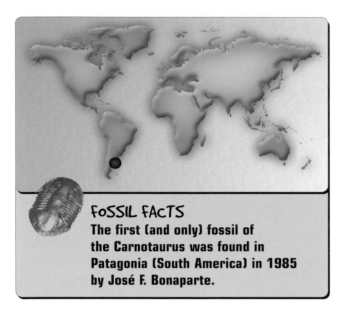

Carnotaurus grew to about 7.6 m (25 ft) long and stood about 4.6 m (15 ft) tall on its hind legs. It moved on two feet and had a long thin tail. We do not know if it had the speed and agility to hunt down prey, but its short, pointed teeth show us it was a meat eater. Instead of hunting, it may have scavenged from the bodies of dead animals.

It had unusually small arms for a **therapod** (probably the tiniest of any meat eater), and its hands had four fingers (one finger being a spike that was directed backwards). These fingers had sharp claws, which it used to hold and tear at its food. The Carnotaurus' hands do not bend and, strangely, seem to be attached directly to its body.

Skull

The skull of Carnotaurus measures only 22 cm (9 in.), showing it had a much shorter snout that other therapods. Its eyes were set facing slightly forwards, so unlike most dinosaurs it may have had partial **binocular vision** (the ability to focus on one object with both eyes, which is very useful for judging distance).

Carnotaurus means 'meat-eating bull'. It was named in 1985 by José F. Bonaparte. It is named from its most notable feature – the two horns located above its eyes, resembling those of a bull. The name comes from the Greek words *carn* (flesh) and *taurus* (bull).

The purpose of these horns is not known. It is possible that they were used for display – for attracting mates, or showing dominance.

This enormous dinosaur lived about 113–91 million years ago in what is now Argentina. It had a small skull, a broad chest and a thin tail.

Appearance

Everything we know about Carnotaurus comes from one find, an almost complete skeleton. The skeleton was so well-preserved, it even kept impressions of the Carnotaurus' rough, bumpy skin all down its right hand side.

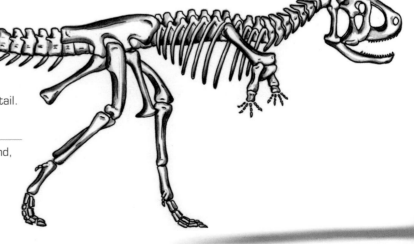

Permian period	Triassic period	Jurassic period	
(290-248 million years ago)	(248-176 million years ago)	(176-130 million years ago)	

Carnotaurus skeleton

MEGA FACTS

- A piece of fossilised skin from the head of a Carnotaurus shows a pattern of small scales, with larger scales covering prominent positions like the snout. These larger scales may have made these areas more colourful, as is quite common in lizards.

- More than five times as big as an African lion.

- Carnotaurus was one of the major villains in Disney's animated film *Dinosaur*.

- Carnotaurus weighed about 1,000 kg (1 ton).

- Carnotaurus featured in the Michael Crichton novel *The lost world*, but didn't make it into the film version — the film-makers opted for a Ceratosaurus instead.

Dinosaur Data

PRONUNCIATION:	**KAR**-NO-**TAWR**-US
SUBORDER:	THERAPODA
FAMILY:	ABELISAURIDAE
DESCRIPTION:	HORNED CARNIVORE
FEATURES:	EYEHORNS, TINY ARMS
DIET:	OTHER DINOSAURS, MAY HAVE SCAVENGED ON DEAD BODIES

SPINOSAURUS

Huge sail-backed predator

Spinosaurus means 'spined lizard'. It was named by Stromer in 1915, after its most unusual feature – a row of high spines running down its backbone, which probably had skin stretched between them to form a 'sail' up to 2 m (6 ft) tall.

The biggest of them all

In February 2006 Spinosaurus was revealed as the biggest meat-eating dinosaur of them all – bigger even than Tyrannosaurus Rex (see page 54) and Giganotosaurus (see page 56)!

This announcement was made based on estimates made from newly-studied Spinosaurus skull and jaw fossils. Scientists worked out that Spinosaurus would have been a massive 17 m (56 ft) long and weighed 7,000–9,000 kg (7–9 tons). (The specimens studied were from a young Spinosaurus, so a fully-grown one might have been even heavier, perhaps up to 20,000kg (20 tons)).

Appearance and diet

Spinosaurus walked on two legs, like other **therapods**, but unlike most therapods had a long and slender snout, resembling the jaws of a crocodile. Their teeth were not the sharp, flesh-ripping scythes of Gigantosaurus and others of its kind, but long, conical and interlocked. This suggests that their main diet may have been fish – in fact, bones from a sawfish were found stuck between a tooth socket and an emerging tooth in one of the Spinosaurus skull fragments.

However, Spinosaurus also had strong arms with which to catch and hold prey on land. It probably lived along the shore, where fish would be abundant. The large, hook-like claw on each of its front limbs could have been used for catching fish as well as gripping and slashing prey.

The sail on its back

Its most unusual feature was the large sail on its back, formed by spines almost 2 m (6 ft) tall. This was most likely used for display purposes, much as a

FOSSIL FACTS

Fossils have been found in Egypt and Morocco. The first specimen was discovered in 1911, in Egypt, by a German geologist and palaeontologist called Ernst Stromer.

peacock uses its colourful tail to attract a mate. The sail would have made the Spinosaurus look bigger – and so more dangerous – to potential attackers. It may also have been used for temperature regulation – the sail would have provided Spinosaurus with an increased surface area, useful for absorbing heat, and for getting rid of surplus body heat.

MEGA FACTS

- Spinosaurus is the main villain of *Jurassic Park III*, in which it battles a Tyrannosaurus Rex and comes out the winner.

- Spinosaurus had a skull 1.75 m (5 ft 9 in.) long. That's as long as a tall human.

- The spines on its back were very flat and bladelike, and at 1.6 m (5 ft), taller than any other dinosaur possessed.

- Comparison of brain to body size suggests Spinosaurus was one of the smarter dinosaurs.

- Given the length of its arms, may have gone on all fours at times.

Dinosaur Data

PRONUNCIATION:	SPINE-O-SAWR-US
SUBORDER:	THERAPOD
FAMILY:	SPINOSAURIDAE
DESCRIPTION:	HUGE CARNIVORE
FEATURES:	LONG JAWS, TALL SAIL ON ITS BACK
DIET:	FISH, PLANT-EATING DINOSAURS

MEGALOSAURUS

Huge bipedal

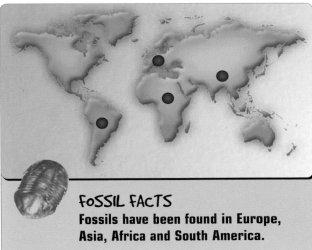

FOSSIL FACTS
Fossils have been found in Europe, Asia, Africa and South America.

This **carnivore** grew to a length of 9 m (30 ft), a height of 3.7 m (12 ft). It was **bipedal**. It had a long tail to help balance out its heavy head.

Its back legs were much longer than its arms. The arms had hands that could have been used for grasping. The legs ended in four-toed feet (one toe was reversed, like all **therapod** dinosaurs). Both fingers and toes had strong, sharp claws.

Diet

Megalosaurus was a powerful hunter, and could attack even the largest prey. It would have hunted plant-eating

Megalosaurus means 'great lizard'. It was named in 1824 and was the first dinosaur to be given a scientific name.

Appearance

No complete skeleton has yet been discovered so we cannot be 100% certain of what it looked like.

Megalosaurus had a big head, and its curved teeth had saw edges well suited to eating meat. Its jaws were very powerful. It had small eyes with bony knobs over the top of them and its head was held up by a strong, short neck.

Dinosaur Data

PRONUNCIATION:	**MEG**-UH-LOW-**SAWR**-US
SUBORDER:	THERAPODA
FAMILY:	MEGALOSAURIDAE
DESCRIPTION:	LARGE BIPEDAL CARNIVORE
FEATURES:	POWERFUL JAWS, BULKY BODY, LARGE HEAD
DIET:	OTHER DINOSAURS

dinosaurs. It probably also scavenged from dead bodies as part of its diet.

Movement

Megalosaurus waddled, rather like a duck, its tail swishing from side to side! Scientists have studied its fossilised footprints, which show that its feet pointed inwards as it walked.

There is fossil evidence to suggest Megalosaurus could actually put on quite a turn of speed when it had to. In 2002, scientists from the University of Cambridge (England) studied fossilised footprints left by Megalosaurus. For about 35 m (115 ft), the footprints looked different to the rest. They were about 3 m (10 ft) apart, and went in a straight line – it looked as if the dinosaur had been placing its feet almost directly beneath itself as it ran.

MEGA FACTS

- Fossilised footprints made by Megalosaurus and another dinosaur called Cetiosaurus have been found in a section of limestone that covers half a square kilometre (a fifth of a square mile).

- In 1676, the thigh bone of a Megalosaurus was found in England. Professors at Oxford University declared it was from a giant man!

- Megalosaurus was one of the more intelligent of the dinosaurs.

At the end of this 35 m (115 ft), the tracks began to change, showing the dinosaur slowing down. In few strides, the prints settled into a new pattern. The footprints were now only 1.3 m (4 ft) apart, and started to look 'pigeon-toed' (with the toes turned in). Using these tracks, scientists estimated that Megalosaurus could run at around 29 km/h (18 mph). It would usually have plodded along at around 7 km/h (4 mph).

TROODON

Intelligent bipedal dinosaur

FOSSIL FACTS
The first fossil was found by Ferdinand V. Hayden in 1855. Fossils have been found in the USA and Canada.

Appearance

Troodon was a **biped** with long hind legs, relatively short arms, a long thin jaw with sharp serrated teeth and a stiff tail that would have helped it balance when running and leaping.

It weighed about 60 kg (175 lb). It was about 3.5 m (12 ft) long and 1 m (3 ft) tall at the hips.

Its long hind legs had large, sickle-shaped claws on the second toes of each foot. Troodon used these claws for kicking into its prey, to cause terrible wounds and prevent it being thrown off as it used its teeth and front claws to bite and tear. The sickle claws were much longer than the other toes' claws and would have been kept

Troodon was discovered by Ferdinand Hayden in 1855 and named by Joseph Leidy in 1856. The name means 'wounding tooth'. It was named after the serrated tooth that was the first fragment of its skeleton to be found.

Troodon tooth

Dinosaur Data

PRONUNCIATION:	**TRUE**-OH-DON
SUBORDER:	THEROPODA
FAMILY:	TROODONTIDAE
DESCRIPTION:	LARGE-EYED INTELLIGENT DINOSAUR
FEATURES:	LARGE BRAIN, PARTIALLY OPPOSABLE THUMBS, SICKLE-SHAPED TOE CLAW, LARGE EYES
DIET:	LIZARDS, SNAKES, SMALL MAMMALS AND OTHER SMALL CREATURES

pointing upwards when running or walking. Its arms had a bird-like wrist joint that allowed them to fold in and back, rather like a bird folds its wings.

Hunting

Troodon had large eyes that would have enabled it to see well in the dark. They were also slightly forward facing which have allowed it limited **binocular vision**.

Troodon had a large brain to body size ratio, strongly suggesting it was one of the most intelligent dinosaurs.

Troodon had partially opposable thumbs, which would have helped it grasp branches and other objects more firmly. The opposable thumb was vital in human evolution as it allowed us to manipulate tools.

Troodon probably hunted at dusk or twilight when its night vision would give it an advantage. Troodon would have hunted small mammals and lizards and perhaps baby dinosaurs.

MEGA FACTS

- One of the first dinosaurs found in North America.

- Troodon may have supplemented its diet with plants, making it an omnivore.

- Fossilised Troodon nests have been found, suggesting that Troodon brooded over its eggs rather like hens.

- Had they not become extinct, dinosaurs like Troodon with their opposable thumbs and large brains might have developed to become intelligent creatures. In the 1980s, palaeontologist Dale Russell worked with artist Ron Sequin to produce a model of an upright dinosaur called Dinosauroid to show what such a creature could have looked like.

- Troody is a robotic Troodon built at MIT, to simulate how these creatures walked.

EORAPTOR

Meat-eating biped

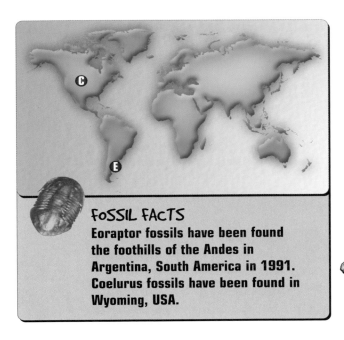

FOSSIL FACTS
Eoraptor fossils have been found the foothills of the Andes in Argentina, South America in 1991. Coelurus fossils have been found in Wyoming, USA.

Dinosaur Data

PRONUNCIATION:	**EE**-OH-**RAP**-TOR
SUBORDER:	THEROPODA
FAMILY:	EORAPTOR
DESCRIPTION:	A SMALL MEAT EATER
FEATURES:	LIGHT-BODY, QUICK MOVEMENT
DIET:	REPTILES, HERBIVOROUS DINOSAURS

Eoraptor is thought to be one of the earliest known dinosaurs. It lived during the late Triassic period, about 228 million years ago.

Eoraptor was about 1 m (3 ft) long. It would have weighed anything between 3 and 15 kg (6 and 33 lb). It had two long legs that enabled it to run quite quickly. It would have needed to run to catch its prey. However, it was probably a scavenger, too.

As well as running upright on its hind legs, Eoraptor also had arms, which were only half the length of its legs. It had sharp claws on each hand that would have been used to catch and tear its prey. Eoraptor was probably an **omnivore**, so it would have eaten plants and tiny mammal-like reptiles and small herbivorous dinosaurs.

Eoraptor's front teeth were leaf-shaped which means that it would have needed to find softer food such as small prey or rotting carcasses of dead dinosaurs.

COELURUS

Hollow tail

Dinosaur Data

PRONUNCIATION:	CEE-LOOR-USS
SUBORDER:	COELUROSAUR
DESCRIPTION:	BIPEDAL MEAT EATER
DIET:	SMALL MAMMALS, FROGS, LIZARDS, AND LARGE INSECTS

MEGA FACTS

- Eoraptor had hollow bones, so its body was very light.

- Eoraptor was no taller than a small child.

- Coelurus was thought by some to be the same as another dinosaur, Ornitholestes.

The slender Coelurus was discovered in the Morrison Formation rocks in Wyoming in the US and named by the famous dinosaur hunter Othniel Marsh in 1879.

At 2 m (6 ft) long and 15 kg (33 lb), Coelurus was quite light for its size because it had hollow bones like birds. Coelurus had a small, low head about 20 cm (8 in.) long on a long and flexible neck. Its tail was very long and very slim, making Coelurus a very elegant creature in appearance. It had strong, long thighs and walked upright.

Living in swampy areas, Coelurus would have hunted small mammals, frogs, lizards and large insects for food.

85

COELOPHYSIS

Meat-eating biped

FOSSIL FACTS
Fossils have been found in the
south-west of the USA.

Like the Eoraptor (see page 84), Coelophysis
moved around on its hind legs in an upright
position. It is believed that it first appeared in the
late Triassic period about 210 million years ago.
It was also one of the earliest known dinosaurs.

Wish bone and tail

An interesting feature of the Coelophysis is that it had a wish
bone (just like a chicken!), which is the earliest example known
in a dinosaur. Another feature that makes the Coelophysis
stand out is the movement of its tail, which was shaped in a
way that allowed the Coelophysis to use it as a rudder when it
was moving, so that it could keep its balance.

Hunting and diet

Coelophysis probably moved around in packs and hunted together. Their teeth were blade-like with fine serrations, suggesting that Coelophysis were predatory dinosaurs. Evidence shows that they caught live prey whenever they had the opportunity and would also have scavenged.

A large number of Coelophysis fossils were found together, supporting the theory that they lived together in a pack. However, some believe that the Coelophysis were gathered together at the water to drink and all died in a flood.

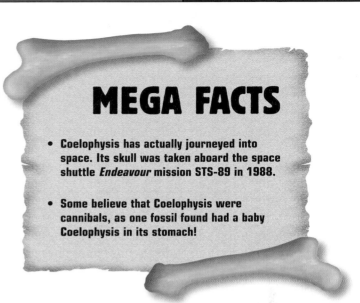

MEGA FACTS

- Coelophysis has actually journeyed into space. Its skull was taken aboard the space shuttle *Endeavour* mission STS-89 in 1988.

- Some believe that Coelophysis were cannibals, as one fossil found had a baby Coelophysis in its stomach!

Dinosaur Data

PRONUNCIATION:	SEE-LAW-**FYS**-ISS
SUBORDER:	THEROPODA
FAMILY:	COELOPHYSIDAE

CARCHARODONTOSAURUS

Jagged-toothed lizard

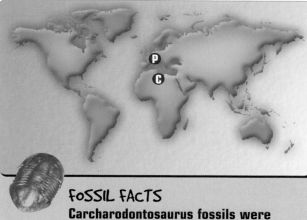

FOSSIL FACTS

Carcharodontosaurus fossils were first discovered by Charles Depéret and J. Savornin in North Africa in 1927. Unfortunately the first fossils were destroyed during World War II. Happily, further fossils were subsequently found in North Africa by paleontologist Paul Sereno in 1996. Procompsognathus fossils have been discovered in Wittenberge, Germany.

Diet

Carcharodontosaurus was a meat eater, with an enormous jaw equipped with many long, serrated teeth each up to 20 cm (8in.) long. It may have hunted in packs and would also have scavenged rotting carcasses. Its long muscular legs would have enabled it to run quite fast, at up to 30 km/h (19 mph) when hunting.

A large meat eater, at 12 m (39 ft) long and weighing 4,000 kg (4 tons), Carcharodontosaurus was nearly as large as Tyrannosaurus Rex (see page 54).

Skull

It was originally believed to have had the longest skull of any **theropod** but this belief was based on investigations of an incomplete fossil. It is now believed that the skull was around 1.6 m (5 ft) long. The largest known therapod skull is actually Gigantosaurus (see page 56) to whom Carcharontosaurus is related.

Permian period	**Triassic period**	**Jurassic period**
(290-248 million years ago)	(248-176 million years ago)	(176-130 million years ago)

PROCOMPSOGNATHUS

Small, speedy therapod

At 2–3 kg (4–7 lb) Procompsognathus was about the same weight as a pet cat but, at 1.3 m (4 ft) nose to tail tip it was about twice as long.

Appearance and diet

Fast on its feet it caught insects, lizards, bugs and newly-hatched reptiles to eat, chewing them up with its many small teeth. Procompsognathus walked upright on its long hind legs, balancing with its long stiff pointed tail which it held off the ground. Its arms were short with large four-fingered clawed hands which it would have used for grabbing its prey.

It is believed that Procompsognathus could inflict a poisonous bite although this has not been proved.

Dinosaur Data

PRONUNCIATION:	PRO-COMP-SON-AY-THUS
SUBORDER:	THERAPODA
DESCRIPTION:	FAST-MOVING, MEAT-EATING
	BIPED

HERRERASAURUS

Herrera's reptile

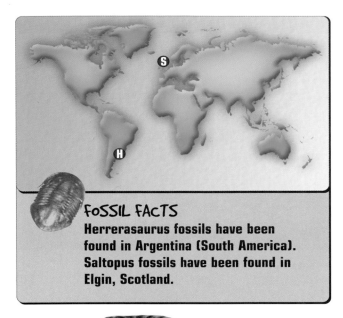

FOSSIL FACTS
Herrerasaurus fossils have been found in Argentina (South America). Saltopus fossils have been found in Elgin, Scotland.

Dinosaur Data

PRONUNCIATION:	HE-RAY-RAAR-SORE-USS
SUBORDER:	THERAPODA
DESCRIPTION:	FAST-MOVING MEAT EATER

It had strong hind legs with short thighs and long feet, indicating that it was a fast runner. Its long, flexible tail would have enabled it to balance and turn quickly as it ran. As a hunter it would have preyed on small and medium-sized dinosaurs using its long jaw and sharp teeth to tear and chew the meat.

A specimen of Herrerasaurus is displayed at the Chicago Field Museum of Natural History.

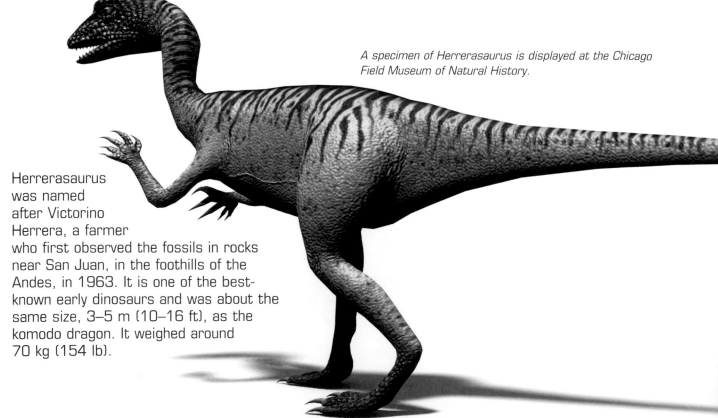

Herrerasaurus was named after Victorino Herrera, a farmer who first observed the fossils in rocks near San Juan, in the foothills of the Andes, in 1963. It is one of the best-known early dinosaurs and was about the same size, 3–5 m (10–16 ft), as the komodo dragon. It weighed around 70 kg (154 lb).

SALTOPUS

Leaping foot

Saltopus is one of the smallest dinosaurs ever found at only 25 cm (10 in.) tall and measuring around 60 cm (2 ft) nose to tail tip.

Saltopus probably weighed about 1–2 kg (2–4 lb). It was still a meat eater, with a jaw full of sharp teeth and five clawed fingers on each hand, scavenging rotting carcasses of dinosaurs killed by larger predators or catching insects.

It could move quite fast on its hind legs, using its long tail to balance as it walked or ran. This would have helped it with catching insects and small reptiles for food.

Dinosaur Data

PRONUNCIATION:	SALL-TOE-PUSS
SUBORDER:	THEROPODA
FAMILY:	SALTOPODDIDAE
DESCRIPTION:	SMALL MEAT EATER

COLOUR AND CAMOUFLAGE

Snake

Scientists have discovered that dinosaurs were covered with tough, scaly skin like modern reptiles.

Skin colour

We don't know what colour their skin was, because animals' skin colours are produced by organic pigments which are not preserved in the process of fossilisation. But we know that dinosaurs were very visual animals, with large nerves and brain centres for vision, so they probably responded to colour and had lots of colours on them. Like animals

today, dinosaurs probably used colour to conceal, disguise, and identify themselves.

Modern animals make use of visual display as a means of communication in mati, aggressive behaviour, and territorial defence, and there is no reason to suppose that dinosaurs were any different.

Camouflage

It is likely that some dinosaurs had protective colouring, such as pale undersides to reduce shadows and spotty patterns, known as 'camouflage', to make them

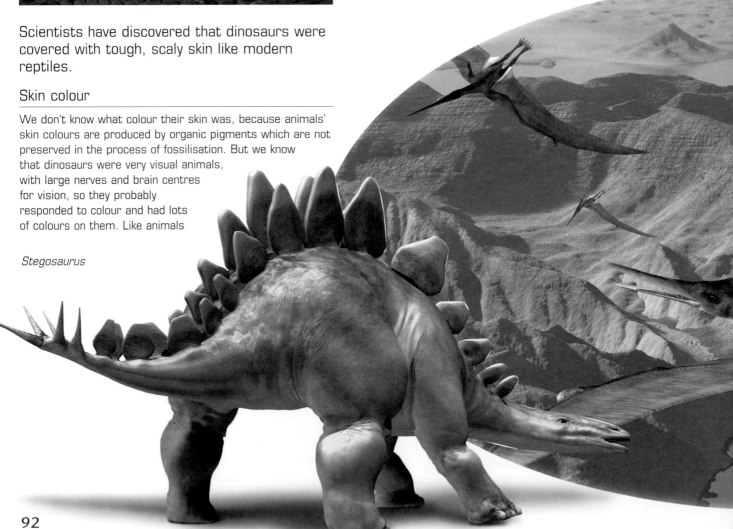

Stegosaurus

less visible among the plants. A medium-sized hadrosaur like Kritosaurus, which was similar to Gryposaurus (see page 182) probably had a mixed skin colour of greens and yellows, to camouflage its low body in the vegetation. If it sensed danger, it probably would have frozen still in order to blend into the forest and remain unnoticed. Woodland species may have been mottled green, brown, and yellow. Open country dwellers may have had patterns of black and white to hide body shape. Young were probably more brightly coloured than older ones. Maybe they had colourful feathers too – we know some small meat eaters had feathers.

Those dinosaurs that had enough armour, such as the stegosaurs and ceratopsians, may not have needed protective skin colour, but they may have been brightly coloured as a warning to predators. Bright colours in nature normally mean a poisonous species. Big animals don't usually have bright colours – they don't need to hide or show off. Perhaps small dinosaurs were very colourful, like birds.

Display

Colour could also have been used by dinosaurs as part of a display for finding a mate. Like animals today, colouring announces that the male is ready to breed and helps females to make their choice of partner. Stegosaurus (see page 116) had two rows of diamond-shaped plates along its back. Each plate was filled with hundreds of tiny blood vessels, so if the creature needed to cool down it could

Gryposaurus

pump blood into the plates, turning them bright red. This colour could have been used as part of a mating display. Simlarly, some dinosaurs probably used their gigantic head crests and horns for mating instead of defence. A network of blood vessels allowed them to flush their crests with blood, perhaps creating a colourful display that would help attract a mate.

Pteranodons

BRACHIOSAURUS

Tree-top grazing giant

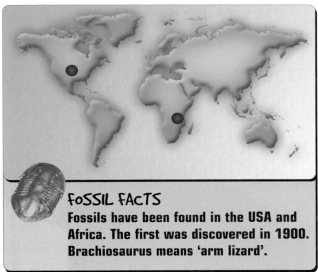

FoSSIL FACTS
Fossils have been found in the USA and Africa. The first was discovered in 1900. Brachiosaurus means 'arm lizard'.

GIANT PLANT EATERS

thought Brachiosaurus actually had two brains, the second near the hip area – but current thinking is that this was simply an enlargement in the spinal cord.

Habitat

At first, scientists believed it must have been an aquatic dinosaur, spending all its time in the water and using its long neck and the nostrils on top of its head as a kind of snorkel for breathing. However, studies showed that water pressure would have stopped Brachiosaurus from breathing properly when submerged.

Brachiosaurus was named in 1903 and gets its name from its long front limbs. It was 25 m (82 ft) long and 15 m (49 ft) high.

For many years it was thought to be the world's biggest dinosaur, but recent discoveries – such as Argentinosaurus (see page 96) – were proved to be bigger in terms of sheer mass.

Appearance and diet

Brachiosaurus walked on four legs, had a long neck, tiny head and a comparatively short, thick tail. It had chisel-like teeth to nip leaves and fruit from the trees. It had nostrils on top of its head, which meant it could eat almost constantly without interfering with its breathing. It swallowed its food whole, without chewing.

To help with its digestion, brachiosaurus swallowed stones. These stayed in its gizzard. Tough leaves and plant fibres would be ground up by the stones as they went through.

Circulation system

To pump blood all the way up its long neck to its tiny brain, Brachiosaurus had to have a powerful heart and broad, strong blood vessels, with valves to prevent the blood obeying gravity and flowing backwards. Scientists once

Permian period	Triassic period	Jurassic period	Cretaceous period
(290-248 million years ago)	(248-176 million years ago)	(176-130 million years ago)	(130-65 million years ago)

Dinosaur Data

PRONUNCIATION:	BRACK-EE-OH-**SAWR**-US
SUBORDER:	SAUROPODOMORPHA
FAMILY:	BRACHIOSAURIDAE
DESCRIPTION:	LONG-NECKED **HERBIVORE**
FEATURES:	HUGE FRONT LIMBS; TINY HEAD
DIET:	HERBIVORE

MEGA FACTS

- Brachiosaurus may well have lived to be 100 years old.

- It probably travelled in herds.

- Brachiosaurus needed to consume 200 kg (440 lb) of food *every day* to fuel its massive body.

- It weighed 20 times as much as a large elephant!

- A full-size replica of a Brachiosaurus skeleton is mounted in O'Hare International Airport, Chicago.

Scientists now believe that Brachiosaurus lived completely on land. Although their fossilised footprints have been found beside shorelines (they probably went there to drink) they have also been found in areas that 156–145 million years ago would have had very little water.

In 2003, a computer simulation run by Dr Donald Henderson in Canada, showed that Brachiosaurus would have floated rather than sunk if it had fallen into deep water – its hollow backbones would have helped it to float, though it would probably have rolled onto its sides in the water rather than staying upright.

ARGENTINOSAURUS

Gigantic long-necked herbivore

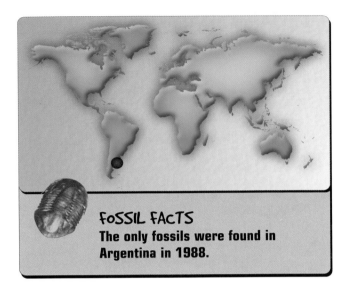

FOSSIL FACTS
The only fossils were found in Argentina in 1988.

Argentinosaurus means 'lizard from Argentina'. It was named in 1993 by **palaeontologists** José F. Bonaparte and Rodolfo Coria after the country where it was found.

Appearance

Argentinosaurus may have grown up to 40 m (130 ft) long, 21 m (69 ft) tall and about 9 m (30 ft) wide and weighed 90–110 tons (90,000–110,000 kg).

An entire skeleton has yet to be discovered. Only about 10% of the Argentinosaurus skeleton was found, and nothing at

all from its neck or tail. Scientists used the bones that *were* found to work out which other dinosaurs Argentinosaurus was related to. They then made their 'best guesses' at its appearance based on what those other dinosaurs looked like.

It would have looked very similar to a Brachiosaurus (see page 94) with a long tail, and a tiny triangular-shaped head on the end of its long neck. It would have needed a big, powerful heart to pump blood all the way up that long neck to its tiny brain.

Backbone

Scientists think its backbone worked in a special way to support the vast weight of the animal. The backbones interlinked to

Dinosaur Data

PRONUNCIATION:	AHY-GEN-**TEEN**-OH-**SAWR**-US
SUBORDER:	SAUROPODOMORPHA
FAMILY:	TITANOSAURIA
DESCRIPTION:	GIGANTIC LONG-NECKED HERBIVORE
FEATURES:	SPECIAL INTERLOCKING BACKBONE, LONG NECK
DIET:	MOSTLY CONIFERS, ALSO FLOWERS, FRUIT AND SEEDS

Permian period	Triassic period	Jurassic period	
(290-248 million years ago)	**(248-176 million years ago)**	**(176-130 million years ago)**	

make the whole back into a sort of bridge of bone. Curiously for such a big animal, the bones were hollow – perhaps they evolved that way to reduce weight and let Argentinosaurus move its vast bulk around more quickly.

Diet

Argentinosaurus was a herbivore, living on plants. It would have had to eat a huge amount to keep its massive body going, and probably spent most of its waking moments eating. Luckily, the area where it lived was full of lush vegetation. This is the area we now call Patagonia. It would have eaten mostly conifers, seeds, fruit and flowering plants.

The biggest animal ever to live is a modern day giant, the Blue Whale. Argentinosaurus *was* the biggest animal that ever lived on land, though. Its relative, Seismosaurus (see page 102) was actually longer, but less tall, wide and heavy.

Argentinosaurus reigns supreme – at least until the next 'big' discovery!

MEGA FACTS

- A single vertebra (backbone) from Argentinosaurus is taller than a child and measures 1.5m (5 ft) across!

- Argentinosaurus was preyed on by the massive meat eater Giganotosaurus (see page 56) and perhaps an even larger recently-discovered meat eater – *Mapusaurus Roseae*, that hunted in packs!

- Thanks to its long neck, Argentinosaurus would have no trouble looking in at a third or fourth storey window.

- In its 'teenage' years when it was growing fastest, Argentinosaurus could gain about 45 kg (100 lb) a day!

- Argentinosaurus was as long as four buses!

DIPLODOCUS

Gigantic long-necked herbivore

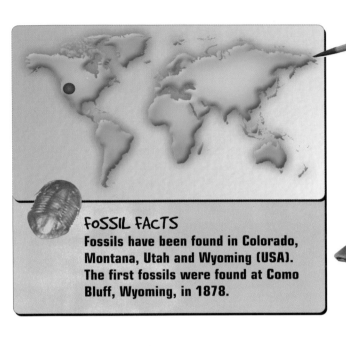

FOSSIL FACTS
Fossils have been found in Colorado, Montana, Utah and Wyoming (USA). The first fossils were found at Como Bluff, Wyoming, in 1878.

Diplodocus means 'double beamed lizard'. It was named in 1878, by Othniel Charles Marsh. The name comes from an unusual feature of the bones in the middle of its tail, where twin extensions of protruding bone run backward and forward. They would have protected blood vessels in the tail if it dragged on the floor, or if the dinosaur pressed its tail against the floor to help balance while rearing on its back legs.

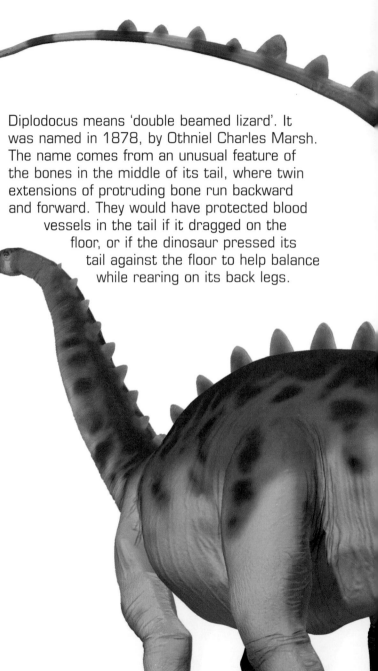

Diplodocus skeleton

Appearance

Diplodocus was one of the longest land animals that ever lived. At 27 m (89 ft) long it was a true giant. It stood around 6 m (20 ft) high at the hip and weighed 10,000–11,000 kg (10–11 tons). Diplodocus had hollow bones and so it weighed only an eighth of the similar-sized Brachiosaurus (see page 94).

Much of its length was accounted for by its long neck and even longer whip-like tail. Its head was tiny, with an elongated snout and nostril on the top of the skull.

In 1990, a new Diplodocus skeleton was found with skin impressions. This suggests diplodocus had row of spines down its back.

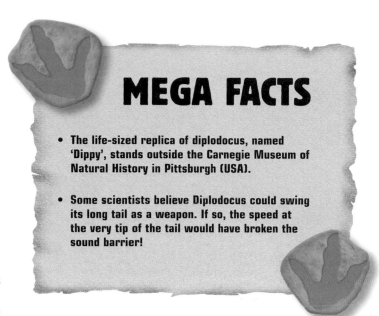

MEGA FACTS

- The life-sized replica of diplodocus, named 'Dippy', stands outside the Carnegie Museum of Natural History in Pittsburgh (USA).

- Some scientists believe Diplodocus could swing its long tail as a weapon. If so, the speed at the very tip of the tail would have broken the sound barrier!

Brain

Diplodocus had a brain the size of a fist. It was once thought that Diplodocus had two brains, one in the skull and one close to the base of the spine. Actually, this second 'brain' was simply a concentration of nerves that helped to control the back legs and tail.

Scientists believe Diplodocus could not lift its head very far from the ground. The longer neck may have allowed Diplodocus to push its neck and head a good distance into overgrown forest areas to find food. It could also swing the neck from side to side, allowing it to graze on a wide area without actually moving. Scientists think that Diplodocus would have spent almost every waking moment eating, just to keep its massive body going.

It was a **quadruped**. Each pillar-like leg had five toes, and one toe on each foot had a thumb claw, which might have been used for self-defence.

Diet

Diplodocus was a **herbivore**. Its main food would have been conifer leaves and ferns. Its simple, peg-like teeth could strip soft foliage like ferns but couldn't chew them up. Diplodocus swallowed small stones (called gastroliths) to help grind up its food in its stomach.

Dinosaur Data

PRONUNCIATION:	DIP-**LOD**-OH-KUS
SUBORDER:	SAUROPODOMORPHA
FAMILY:	DILODOCIDAE
DESCRIPTION:	LONG-NECKED HERBIVORE
FEATURES:	LONG NECK, WHIPLASH TAIL, HOLLOW BONES, TINY HEAD
DIET:	FERNS AND CONIFERS

APATOSAURUS

Formerly known as Brontosaurus

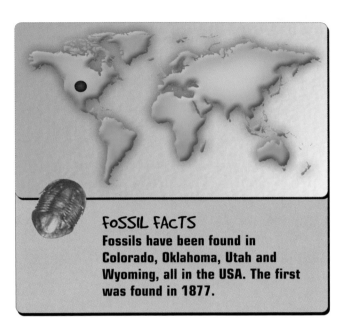

FOSSIL FACTS
Fossils have been found in Colorado, Oklahoma, Utah and Wyoming, all in the USA. The first was found in 1877.

Apatosaurus means 'deceptive lizard'. In 1877, American **palaeontologist** Othniel C. Marsh described and named a dinosaur called Apatosaurus. In 1879, he described and named another set of dinosaur remains, and – believing them to be from a different creature – christened them Brontosaurus.

Appearance

In 1903, it was discovered that Brontosaurus was in fact simply a fully-grown Apatosaurus! However, the name Brontosaurus was not officially removed from lists until 1974, and it is still popular with many people.

Apatosaurus was some 21–27 m (69–90 ft) long, 3–4.6 m (10–15 ft) tall at the hip and weighed 27,000 kg (27 tons). Its head was tiny at only 60 cm (2 ft) in length. Its long neck had 15 vertebrae, and a long, whip-like tail which accounted for 15 m (50 ft) of its whole length. In the front part of its jaw were peg-like teeth, ideal for stripping leaves and browsing on vegetation. Apatosaurus would have had to eat almost constantly when awake – fortunately, nostrils placed on the top of the skull meant it could eat and breathe at the same time.

Apatosaurus swallowed its food without chewing it, and to help with its digestion, it swallowed stones which stayed in its gizzard. Stones swallowed for this purpose are called gastroliths.

A study in 1999 used computer modelling to test the mobility of the neck of Apatosaurus. The results showed that they could not have lifted their heads any higher than 3–4m (10–13 ft) (just a little higher than their backs), and must most of the time have held their heads downwards or straight out. (They could move their heads freely from side to side, though.)

Dinosaur Data

PRONUNCIATION:	A-**PAT**-OH-**SAWR**-US
SUBORDER:	SAUROPODA
FAMILY:	DIPLODOCIDAE
DESCRIPTION:	LARGE, SLOW-MOVING HERBIVORE
FEATURES:	THICK LEGS, TINY HEAD, LONG NECK, LONG THIN TAIL
DIET:	HERBIVORE: LEAVES, PLANTS, MOSSES

The biggest predator around at the time, Allosaurus (see page 72), was only 4.6 m (15 ft) tall – an Apatosaurus whose head was raised even by this limited amount would place its head 5.4 m (18 ft) off the ground, making it almost impossible for the **carnivore** to attack its head and neck.

Like other **sauropods**, Apatosaurus young hatched from huge eggs. It is assumed that Apatosaurus laid their eggs as they walked, and did not take care of their eggs.

Apatosaurus

MEGA FACTS

- Brain the size of a large apple.

- In the 1933 film *King Kong*, an Apatosaurus was depicted as a bloodthirsty carnivore – quite unlike the gentle plant-eating giant it really was.

- Apatosaurus had thick skin to protect it. Just as well – one of its vertebrae was found with Allosaurus tooth marks in it!

- Fossilised Apatosaurus footprints have been found that measured more than a metre across!

Apatosaurus skeleton

SEISMOSAURUS

Giant whip-tailed herbivore

Seismosaurus means 'earthquake lizard' or 'earth shaker lizard', named because a creature of its fantastic size must have surely shaken the Earth as it walked. It was discovered in 1979, and described and named by David D. Gillette in 1991. Because of its huge size, and the rocks in which it was found, it took 13 years to excavate.

Seismosaurus is currently thought to be the longest animal that ever lived. Its length was estimated originally at around 52 m (170 ft) – in 2004, this was revised to 33.5 m (110 ft). This still leaves Seismosaurus at the top of the 'longest dinosaur' list, and just ahead of the previous longest-ever animal, the blue whale (30.5 m or 100 ft). It probably weighed nearly 45,000 kg (45 tons).

All our information about Seismosaurus comes from the fossilised bones from the hip and part of the back, which were found in 1979. Found mingled with the fossilised bones were the fossilised remains of more than 200 'gastroliths' – small stones that Seismosaurus swallowed to help it digest its food. It is possible that the death of this specimen was caused when it swallowed a particularly large stone, which stuck in its throat and blocked its airway.

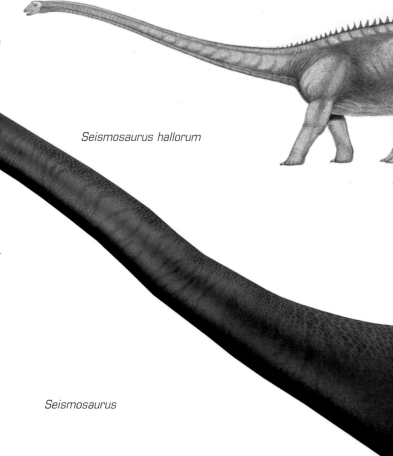

Seismosaurus hallorum

Seismosaurus

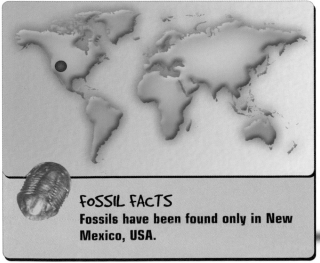

FOSSIL FACTS
Fossils have been found only in New Mexico, USA.

Appearance

Seismosaurus would have looked very like a large Diplodocus (see page 98), and may not have been much taller, as it had short legs compared to its body length. It had four pillar-like legs with five-toed feet like an elephant, a long neck, and a long, thin tail to counterbalance neck and head. Its head was tiny compared to its length, and housed a very small brain.

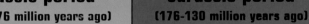

| **Permian period** (290-248 million years ago) | **Triassic period** (248-176 million years ago) | **Jurassic period** (176-130 million years ago) | **Cretaceous period** (130-88 million years ago) |

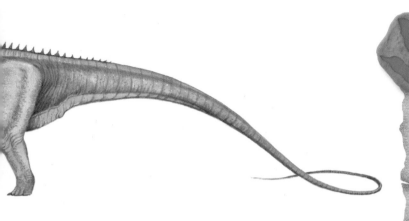

MEGA FACTS

- Probably hatched from eggs like other sauropods.

- Seismosaurus may have lived to be 100 years old.

- Seismosaurus remains are so similar to those of Diplodocus, some scientists think Seismosaurus may not be a separate type of dinosaur at all, but a big new version of Diplodocus.

It had peg-like teeth in the front part of its mouth, ideally suited for stripping the leaves from trees and grazing on plants. It had nostrils on the top of its skull, which allowed it to eat and breathe at the same time. It may have used the whip-like tail for protection.

Seismosaurus' long neck would have usually been held parallel to the ground. It might have allowed the creature to poke its head into dense forest areas to reach leaves otherwise inaccessible to the bulky dinosaurs, or maybe to eat soft **pterodophytes** that grew in wet areas too swampy to enter safely. Its main diet item was probably conifers, huge forests of which flourished in its time.

Dinosaur Data

PRONUNCIATION:	SIZE-MOH-**SAWR**-US
SUBORDER:	SAUROPODOMORPHA
FAMILY:	DIPLODOCIDAE
DESCRIPTION:	INCREDIBLY LONG HERBIVORE
FEATURES:	LONG NECK, TINY HEAD, WHIP-LIKE TAIL
DIET:	LEAVES, FERNS, MOSSES

103

HADROSAURUS

Duck-billed browsing herbivore

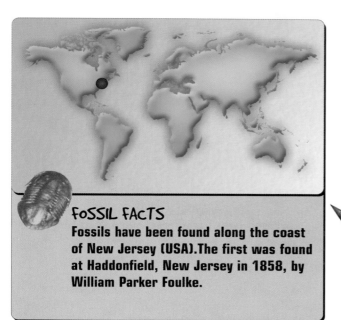

FOSSIL FACTS
Fossils have been found along the coast of New Jersey (USA). The first was found at Haddonfield, New Jersey in 1858, by William Parker Foulke.

Appearance and diet

Hadrosaurus was a herbivore that browsed along the shrub lands and marshes of the Atlantic coast of America 84–71 million years ago. It had a bulky body, stiff tail, and hoof-like nails on its four feet. It was a good swimmer, and may have ventured substantial distances from shore; it could also have spent time in the warm waters. It grew to between 7–10 m (23–30 ft) in length, and 3–4 m (10–13 ft) high – taller than a house if it stood on its back legs! It weighed 1,900 kg (4,000 lb).

Hadrosaurus means 'heavy lizard'. It was studied and named by **palaeontologist** Joseph Leidy in 1858.

When Hadrosaurus was discovered, it was the most complete dinosaur skeleton that had been found. During the 1800s, various specimens of fossilised bones unlike those of any living animal, and much, much bigger, had been found in Europe and North America.

In 1841, Dr Richard Owen, a British authority on anatomy, suggested these bones belonged to a group of large reptiles, all of which had completely died out long ago. It was he who first coined the name 'dinosaurs', meaning 'terrible lizards'. Until Hadrosaurus came along, though, no one was able to say what one of these 'dinosaurs' would have looked like.

The remains dug up in 1858 included, for the first time, enough of a dinosaur's skeleton to document its anatomy. It was also the first dinosaur fossil ever mounted and put on display in a museum. The study of dinosaurs became a well-respected science.

Hadrosaurus

Statue of Hadrosaurus

MEGA FACTS

- Even though Hadrosaurus had a whole dinosaur family named after it, no Hadrosaurus skull has ever been discovered. The shape of its head is deduced from the skulls of other duck-billed dinosaurs.

- In October 2003, a life-size statue of Hadrosaurus, cast in bronze, was unveiled in Haddonfield, close to the place the first Hadrosaurus was found.

- State Official – in 1991, Hadrosaurus became the official 'state dinosaur' of New Jersey.

Its back legs were longer than its front legs, and this at first led scientists to believe it spent most of its time on its hind legs, in a kind of 'kangaroo-like' stance. We now know that it spent most of its time on all fours. The most recent evidence suggests that Hadrosaurus held its whole rear body aloft, to balance it as it leaned its upper body forward in movements similar to those of modern birds. The front limbs would have been used for foraging.

Dinosaur Data

PRONUNCIATION:	**HAD**-ROW-**SAWR**-US
SUBORDER:	ORNITOPODA
FAMILY:	HADROSAURIDAE
DESCRIPTION:	MASSIVE DUCK-BILLED HERBIVORE
FEATURES:	BULKY BODY, TOOTHLESS BEAK
DIET:	LEAVES, TWIGS

MELANOROSAURUS

Giant herbivorous dinosaur

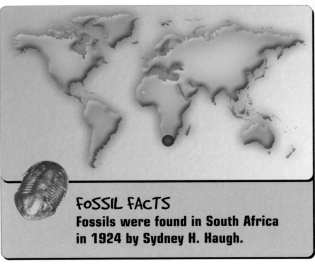

FOSSIL FACTS
Fossils were found in South Africa in 1924 by Sydney H. Haugh.

Melanorosaurus

Melanorosaurus means 'Black Mountain lizard' and comes from the Greek words *melanos* (black), *oros* (mountain) and *sauros* (lizard). It was named by the British **palaeontologist** Sydney H. Haugh in 1924 after the Thaba Nyama or Black Mountain in South Africa where the fossil was found.

Appearance

Melanorosaurus lived in the early Triassic period. At 12 m (39 ft) long, 4.3 m (14 ft) tall and probably weighing around 2250 kg (5,000 lb), it was the largest land animal of its time.

Like all **sauropods**, Melanorosaurus was herbivorous and had a bulky body, long neck and tail, a relatively small skull and brain and erect limbs reminiscent of the limbs of elephants. For some time it was believed that Melanorosaurus was a **quadruped**, as were many of the giant sauropods.

However, recently scientists have speculated that the sturdy hind limbs with their strong, dense bones could have enabled the creature to walk on its two hind legs, a theory that is given extra weight by the fact that the fore limbs were rather shorter than the hind limbs.

This ability to walk on two legs would make it a facultative **biped**, a creature that *could* walk on two legs but didn't have to – it may well have taken advantage of this ability to rear up on its hind legs in its quest for tasty leaves!

Diet

Melanorosaurus' diet would have consisted of branches, leaves and twigs, with its height and long neck allowing it to easily reach the tops of trees. Taking large mouthfuls of food at a time, it would use its serrated leaf-shaped teeth to snap off branches and then chew the vegetation quite effectively before swallowing. Its long neck meant it could browse over a sizeable area by just moving its head and neck, this allowed it to reduce the amount of energy it would have to use up in moving – important when considering how much energy from plants it would take to maintain such a large body.

MEGA FACTS

- Biggest dinosaur of the Triassic era! At 12 m (39 ft) long, Melanorosaurus was the largest dinosaur of its day – only in the Cretaceous period and later have larger dinosaurs been found.

- So far no Melanorosaurus skull has been discovered. However it is believed that its skull would have been very similar in shape to those of the other giant sauropods, many of whose skulls have been found.

- Whilst its limbs had dense bones, its spinal bones and vertebrae had hollows to reduce their weight.

Dinosaur Data

PRONUNCIATION:	MEL-UH-**NOR**-UH-**SAWR**-US
SUBORDER:	SAUROPODOMORPHA
FAMILY:	MELANOROSAURIDAE
DESCRIPTION:	GIANT LONG-NECKED **HERBIVORE**
FEATURES:	LONG NECK AND TAIL, BULKY BODY, LEAF-SHAPED SERRATED TEETH
DIET:	BRANCHES, LEAVES AND TWIGS

SALTASAURUS

Armour-plated herbivore

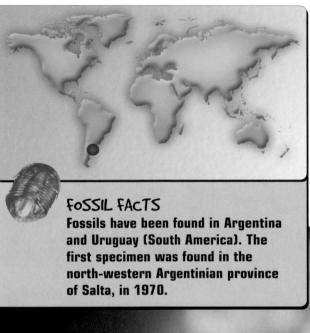

FOSSIL FACTS
Fossils have been found in Argentina and Uruguay (South America). The first specimen was found in the north-western Argentinian province of Salta, in 1970.

Dinosaur Data

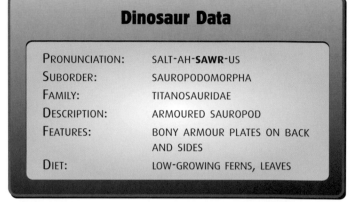

PRONUNCIATION:	SALT-AH-**SAWR**-US
SUBORDER:	SAUROPODOMORPHA
FAMILY:	TITANOSAURIDAE
DESCRIPTION:	ARMOURED SAUROPOD
FEATURES:	BONY ARMOUR PLATES ON BACK AND SIDES
DIET:	LOW-GROWING FERNS, LEAVES

Saltasaurus means 'lizard from Salta'. It is named after the Argentinian province of Salta where it was found by José Bonaparte and Jaime Powell in 1980.

Appearance

Saltsaurus was a **sauropod**, 12 m (40 ft) long and weighed 7,000 kg (7 tons). It had a bulky body, four stout legs ending in five-toed feet, a long neck ending in a tiny head, and a stout tail that tapered to whiplash thinness.

Its neck was shorter than that of most sauropods, but would still have helped it to feed on vegetation out of the reach of shorter **herbivores**. It had blunt teeth, in the back part of its mouth only. Some scientists believe it could rear up on its hind legs for short periods of time, perhaps using its tail for extra support and balance.

Saltasaurus lived about 70–65 million years ago. In most parts of the world at this time, sauropod dinosaurs were giving way to the more successful duck-billed dinosaurs.

South America, though, was an island continent and life evolved there somewhat differently. The duckbills never made much of an impression there, and sauropods continued to evolve there long after they had largely died out elsewhere.

MEGA FACTS

- A large nesting ground discovered in 1997 may have belonged to Saltasaurus. Remains showed that several hundred holes and been dug and eggs about 11–12 cm (4–5 in.) in diameter laid in them. The nests were then buried under dirt and vegetation to conceal them from predators.

- Communal nest building shows that Saltasaurus probably lived and travelled in herds.

- Saltasaurus eggs had a shell 6 mm (¼ in.) thick.

Armour plating

This may explain the most distinctive feature of Saltasaurus – unlike any previously-found sauropods, it had armour plating! Its back and sides were covered in circular and oval bony plates, up to 12 cm (5 in.) in diameter. It is thought horns or spikes may have stuck out from these plates, but firm evidence for this is yet to be found.

The discovery of Saltasaurus completely changed the way scientists thought about the sauropods. It had been assumed until then that the sauropods' size alone was enough to protect them from predators – so when Titanosaurus (see page 110) remains were found with armour plates, it had been reclassified as an **ankylosaur**. Saltasaurus showed that a dinosaur could have armour *and* still be a sauropod, and Titanosaurus was returned to the sauropod fold.

TITANOSAURUS

Giant armoured herbivore

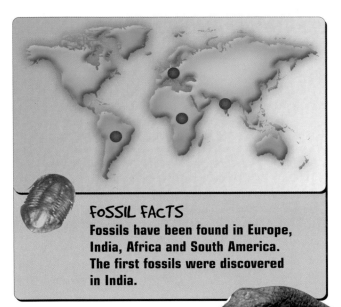

FOSSIL FACTS
Fossils have been found in Europe, India, Africa and South America. The first fossils were discovered in India.

Appearance

Titanosaurus had a bulky body, a long 'whiplash' tail and a tiny head on the end of its long neck. The head was incredibly small compared to the rest of its body, but was quite wide. It had large nostrils, and its nasal bones formed a sort of raised crest on its skull. It had very small teeth.

It grew to around 12–18 m (39–59 ft) in length and about 3–5 m (10–16 ft) tall at the hips. It would have weighed about 14,700 kg (15 tons).

This dinosaur walked on all fours. Its front legs were stout and stocky. Its back legs were longer than the front ones, and Titanosaurus would have been able to rear up onto these strong back legs to reach higher up trees for food. It had a very flexible spine, making rearing up easy.

Titanosaurus means 'titanic lizard'. The dinosaur was named by Richard Lydekker in 1877 – almost 20 years after its remains were first discovered.

Titanosaurus was a **sauropod** dionosaur, like Argentinosaurus (see page 96) and Brachiosaurus (see page 94).

(see page 96) ... (see page 94)

Dinosaur Data

PRONUNCIATION:	TIE-**TAN**-OH-**SAWR**-US
SUBORDER:	SAUROPODA
FAMILY:	TITANOSAURIDAE
DESCRIPTION:	GIANT ARMOURED HERBIVORE
FEATURES:	LONG NECK, FLEXIBLE BACK, ARMOURED SKIN
DIET:	CONIFERS, PALMS, GRASSES

GIANT PLANT EATERS

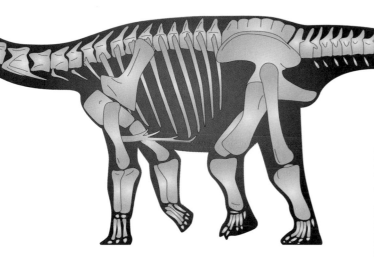

Titanosaurus had a very wide chest, which placed its legs and feet widely apart. Scientists have discovered fossilised footprints (we call these 'fossilised trackways') showing that Titanosaurus tracks are much wider than those of other sauropod dinosaurs.

Fosssilised impressions of Titanosaurus' skin have survived, so we know that it had armour to protect it. Its skin was covered with a pattern of small 'bead-like' scales surrounding larger scales.

Diet

The fossilised remains of Titanosaur dung show that Titanosaurus had quite a broad diet. It ate pretty much any plant material – remains from conifer twigs and leaves, palms and grasses were all found. Titanosaurus lived in herds, browsing from place to place to find fresh vegetation to eat.

Reproduction

Titanosaurus laid eggs, and the whole herd probably shared one large nesting ground, where they dug nests and then buried their eggs under dirt and vegetation. Their eggs would have measured only 11–12 cm (4–5 in.) across.

Latest discoveries

In May 2006, Italian scientists announced the discovery of four well-preserved Titanosaur skeletons in South America. There are skeletons of young Titanosaurs as well as adults.

MEGA FACTS

- Although Titanosaurus eggs were only about 12 cm (5 in.) across, the babies that hatched would grow to be longer than a bus!

- Living in herds would have given Titanosaurus protection against large predators.

111

CAMARASAURUS

Giant herbivore

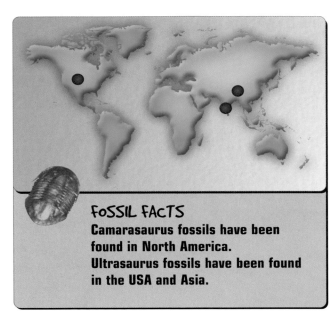

FOSSIL FACTS
Camarasaurus fossils have been found in North America. Ultrasaurus fossils have been found in the USA and Asia.

Dinosaur Data

PRONUNCIATION:	KUH-**MARE**-UH-**SAWR**-US
SUBORDER:	SAUROPODOMORPHA
FAMILY:	CAMARASAURIDAE
DESCRIPTION:	A GIANT HERBIVORE
FEATURES:	SPOON-SHAPED TEETH
DIET:	PLANTS

PLANT EATERS

Camarasaurus lived during the late Jurassic Period, about 155 to 145 million years ago.

Camarasaurus looked very much like Diplodocus with its long neck and tail. It was a giant herbivore, but it wasn't as big as other sauropods. It still weighed up to 20,000 kg (20 tons)!

Its head was small and long, and it had a blunt snout. It had spoon-shaped teeth, which were ideal for munching on leaves and branches.

Camarasaurus fossils have been found in groups with both adult and young together. They probably traveled together in herds like elephants.

112

ULTRASAURUS

Giant herbivore

MEGA FACTS

- Camarasaurus eggs were probably hatched while it was walking along.

- Camarasaurus swallowed stones to help it digest tough plants.

- Despite the large size of Camarasaurus, it had a tiny brain!

- Ultrasaurus had a very powerful heart to pump blood around its massive body.

- Supersaurus probably weighed about 42,000 kg (92,400 pounds)!

Dinosaur Data

PRONUNCIATION:	ULL-TRA-SAW-US
SUBORDER:	SAUROPODOMORPHA
FAMILY:	BRACHIOSAURIDAE (NOT CONFIRMED)
DESCRIPTION:	BIGGEST EVER HERBIVORE
FEATURES:	EXTRA-LONG NECK, TAIL AND HUGE LEGS
DIET:	PLANTS

Ultrasaurus had a very long neck, tail and long legs. It was a herbivore. It was believed to be 18 m (60 ft) tall and 30 m (100 ft) long.

The name was originally given to a sauropod that was found in Colorado, USA, and was then given to another fossil found in Asia. However, it was later discovered that the fossil from Asia was a lot smaller than the first fossil. The discovery in Colorado was one of the largest dinosaur remains ever found and is now officially known as Supersaurus.

COLD-BLOODED CREATURES

People disagree over whether dinosaurs were cold-blooded or warm-blooded. It used to be assumed that dinosaurs were cold-blooded like their reptile ancestors. But some **palaeontologists** have recently argued that at least some dinosaurs were fast, active, competed against hot-blooded mammals, lived in cool areas, were related to birds, and therefore were warm-blooded.

Cold-blooded creatures

Cold-blooded animals, like lizards and snakes, control their body temperature by their behaviour, moving in and out of the sun during the day. This is called the ectothermic ('outside heat') method.

Warm-blooded creatures

Warm-blooded animals (birds and mammals) convert food energy into body heat, the endothermic ('inside heat')

Alligator

method. To cool off, endothermic animals sweat, pant, wallow in water or flap their ears to cool the blood.

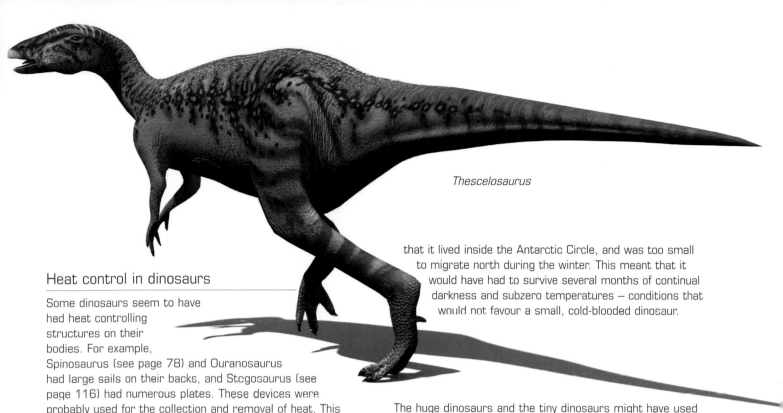

Thescelosaurus

Heat control in dinosaurs

Some dinosaurs seem to have had heat controlling structures on their bodies. For example, Spinosaurus (see page 78) and Ouranosaurus had large sails on their backs, and Stegosaurus (see page 116) had numerous plates. These devices were probably used for the collection and removal of heat. This suggests that they needed these structures to control their body temperature and that they were cold-blooded.

Circulation systems

Laellynasaura was a small but extraordinary dinosaur that lived in dense polar forests near the South Pole during the early Cretaceous period. The amazing aspect of its life was

Laellynasaura

that it lived inside the Antarctic Circle, and was too small to migrate north during the winter. This meant that it would have had to survive several months of continual darkness and subzero temperatures – conditions that would not favour a small, cold-blooded dinosaur.

The huge dinosaurs and the tiny dinosaurs might have used different heat regulation strategies, just as they used different strategies for other aspect of living.

Many of the big dinosaurs, such as Tyrannosaurus Rex (see page 54) and Iguanodon (see page 156), held their heads high above their bodies. To pump blood up to their brains would have required high pressure, far higher than the delicate blood-vessels in their lungs could withstand. Warm-blooded animals deal with this problem by having two blood circuits and internally-divided hearts. Some scientists suggest that large dinosaurs would also have needed a divided heart and must therefore be warm-blooded.

However, whilst it is true that some dinosaurs must have had a divided heart to get blood to their heads, they did not necessarily need to be warm-blooded for this. Perhaps they were a combination of having a warm-blooded heart and lung system, with cold-blooded ways to control temperature. Modern alligators are an example of this, as they have a functionally divided heart but are still cold-blooded.

In 2000 the fossil of a Thescelosaurus (see page 166) was found to have a mammal-like, four-chambered heart. Until then dinosaurs were thought to have had only three-chambered hearts. This suggests not only that Thescelosaurus may have been warm-blooded, but that many other dinosaurs may have been warm-blooded as well.

STEGOSAURUS

Ridge-backed slow-moving herbivore

Its back legs were longer and straighter than its front legs, which stuck out somewhat to the sides. This gave it a downward-sloping shape toward its small, pointed head. Its head was carried close to the ground. It had a toothless, horny beak for cropping vegetation, with small leaf-shaped teeth further back in its cheeks. The back feet had three toes, while the front feet had five — all of them had hoof-like claws.

At the end of its short, flexible tail, Stegosaurus had 1 m (3 ft) spikes, which we now know stuck out sideways rather than upwards. The tail was held horizontal to the ground and could be swung upwards and sideways as a weapon, to defend against predatory dinosaurs.

FOSSIL FACTS
Fossils have been found in the western USA, western Europe, southern India, China and southern Africa.

Stegosaurus was named by Othniel Marsh in 1877. Its name means 'roofed lizard'. It was named after the double row of alternating bony plates embedded in its back (it had 17 plates altogether).

Appearance

Stegosaurus was big, heavy and slow-moving. It grew to between 9–12 m (30–40 ft) long and up to 4 m (13 ft) high. It weighed in at up to 3,000 kg (3 tons).

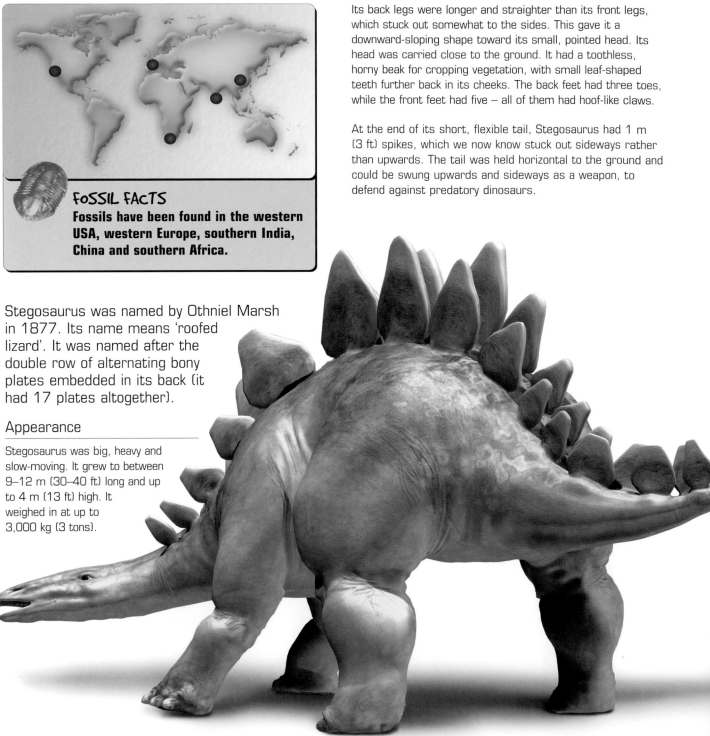

Armoured plates

In addition to its back plates, in 1992 it was discovered that Stegosaurus had chainmail-like armoured plates protecting its throat and hip areas.

The pointy back plates were originally assumed to be armour, for defence against predators. Then it was discovered that they were rather fragile, and not ideally placed for protection. It has been suggested that they may have served only display purposes, such as distinguishing between the male and female of the species – but both male and female Stegosaurus had them.

For a long time, the most popular theory was that the plates were used for regulating body temperature. The most recent theory suggests that the plates were simply used by members of the species to recognise others of their own kind.

Stegosaurus lived in family groups, possibly even in herds. Stegosaurus was not only the largest, but one of the last of the **stegosaurs**. Towards the end of the Jurassic period, a minor mass extinction occurred, and most of the stegosaurs died out.

Dinosaur Data

PRONUNCIATION:	**STEG**-OH-**SAWR**-US
SUBORDER:	THRYREOPHORA
FAMILY:	STEGOSAURIDAE
DESCRIPTION:	SLOW-MOVING, HEAVY HERBIVORE
FEATURES:	SPINES ON BACK, HEAVY SPIKED TAIL
DIET:	LOW-GROWING LEAVES AND PLANTS

MEGA FACTS

- Stegosaurus was nearly as big as a bus – but its brain was only the size of a table-tennis ball, weighing a tiny 71 g (2.4 oz).

- The most complete Stegosaurus yet found was discovered in Colorado in 1992. Its excavators gave it the highly-suitable nickname of 'Spike'.

- Under its feet, Stegosaurus had pads of spongy tissue to help cushion its weight.

Stegosaurus skeleton

117

Tank-like armoured herbivore

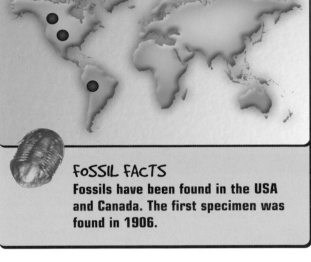

FOSSIL FACTS
Fossils have been found in the USA and Canada. The first specimen was found in 1906.

Ankylosaurus means 'crooked lizard' or 'fused lizard' – the name refers to the fusion of many of its bones to provide extra protection. It was named in 1908.

Appearance

Ankylosaurus was the biggest of the armoured dinosaurs. It died out in the **K-T extinction event** (see page 206) 65 million years ago. Its armour was impressive – back, sides and tail completely protected.

Even its eyelids had plates of bone. In addition to their armour, they had rows of bony spikes that projected from their flanks and bony knobs on its back.

Its body was low-slung, and very wide. It moved slowly on four solid legs, and the back legs were longer than the front ones. Its rather triangular skull was massive.

Four 'horns' stuck out from the back side of the skull, giving extra protection. The skull was also very thick, leaving room for only a small brain. It had a wide muzzle, and a toothless beak of a mouth for grazing. Further back in its mouth were leaf-shaped cheek teeth for grinding up vegetation.

Tail

Ankylosaurus' tail ended in a thick bony 'club', which was supported by the last few vertebrae in the tail, which were fused together to support it. Attached to these vertebrae were thick tendons, enabling the 'club' to be swung with sufficient force to break bones.

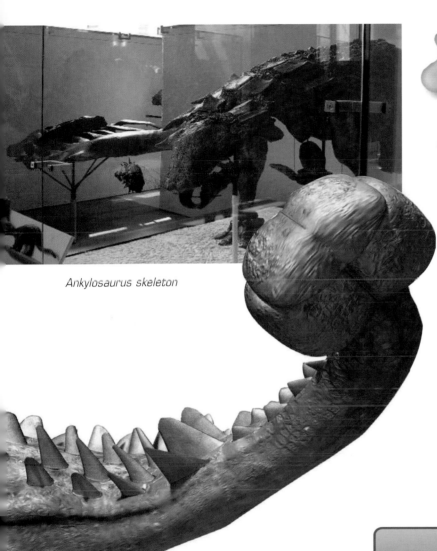

Ankylosaurus skeleton

MEGA FACTS

- In 1996, Ankylosaur trackways (fossilised footprints) were found in Brazil. Speed estimates made using the pattern of these prints revealed that Ankylosaurus could move 'at a decent jog' when needed.

- Ankylosaurus would have had a huge gut, probably with a fermentation chamber to help digest the tough plant material, which would have produced impressive amounts of gas!

mats that would criss-cross from layer to layer. (The pattern of these fibres can still be seen in fossils after millions of years.) This would give the plate great strength in all directions. These 'composite' dinosaur plates were thinner and lighter than the simpler but weaker ones possessed by other species of armoured dinosaur. Layers of them could withstand great amounts of stress – for example, when the Ankylosaurus swung its tail hard in defence.

As a last resort, it could swing the club like a weapon to defend itself. It also probably dropped flat to the ground if attacked, protecting its vulnerable stomach and leaving only its heavily-armoured areas available to its attacker.

Armour structure

In 2004, a study showed that Ankylosaurus' armour had a complex structure, with collagen fibres interwoven in the bone calcium of the plates, forming

Dinosaur Data

PRONUNCIATION:	**ANG**-KI-LO-**SAWR**-US
SUBORDER:	THYREOPHORA
FAMILY:	ANKYLOSAURIDAE
DESCRIPTION:	ARMOUR-PLATED HERBIVORE
FEATURES:	CLUB-LIKE TAIL; HEAVILY ARMOURED BACK AND SIDES
DIET:	LOW-LYING PLANTS

KENTROSAURUS

Slow and spiky herbivore

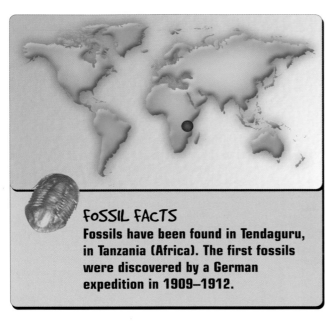

FOSSIL FACTS
Fossils have been found in Tendaguru, in Tanzania (Africa). The first fossils were discovered by a German expedition in 1909–1912.

Dinosaur Data

PRONUNCIATION:	**KEN**-TROH-**SAWR**-US
FAMILY:	STEGOSAURIDAE
DESCRIPTION:	PLATED AND SPIKED HERBIVORE
FEATURES:	ROW OF LONG SHARP SPIKES DOWN BACK AND TAIL
DIET:	FERNS, LOW-GROWING RIVERSIDE PLANTS

Kentrosaurus means 'spiked lizard' or 'pointed lizard'. It was first described and named by Edwin Hennig in 1915.

Appearance

It is named after the dramatic double row of bony spikes that ran from halfway down its back to the end of its tail, standing almost upright in a zigzag arrangement. Each spike was around 30 cm (12 in.) high. At the end of its strong, thick tail it had two pairs of sharp spikes, each nearly 1 m (3 ft) long. It would defend itself against predators by swinging its tail like a weapon.

Above the row of spikes, it had nine pairs of small bony plates sticking up along its upper back, shoulders and neck. These plates contained blood vessels. They were too small to help it regulate its body temperature (as other dinosaurs with larger back plates may have done) but may have been used for display

as well as defence. If used for display, they were probably brightly coloured.

It grew between 2.5 m (8 ft) and 5 m (16 ft) in length. Its height was around 1.8 m (6 ft), and it carried its long, powerful tail higher than its head, which was held low to the ground.

Permian period	Triassic period	Jurassic period	
(290-248 million years ago)	(248-176 million years ago)	(176-130 million years ago)	

Diet

It had a tiny, narrow head ending in a toothless beak. Small teeth further back in its cheeks helped it to mash up the ferns and lush riverside plants that it grazed on. The area where Kentrosaurus fossils were discovered would have been close to a large river 156–150 million years ago when Kentrosaurus lived. Scientists believe it would have grazed the riverbanks for its food.

Its back legs were twice as long as its front legs, and it may have been able to stand up for short periods of time on just its back legs, to reach higher-up vegetation such as leaves.

There is strong evidence that Kentrosaurus moved and lived in herds.

MEGA FACTS

- Kentrosaurus was once believed to have two brains! Scientists now know that this second brain was merely a nerve cluster, which controlled the tail and hind legs (see page 98).

- An almost-complete Kentrosaurus skeleton (one of the only two ever found) at one time stood in the Humboldt Museum at the University of Berlin. During World War II, the museum was bombed and practically all the bones lost.

- Its olfactory bulbs (the area of the brain controlling smell) were very well-developed, so it had a keen sense of smell.

121

EDMONTONIA

Spiny armoured herbivore

FOSSIL FACTS
Fossils have been found in Alberta (Canada) and Montana, South Dakota and Texas (all in the USA). The first specimen was found by George Paterson in 1924.

Edmontonia means 'from Edmonton'. It was named in 1928 by C. M. Sternberg, and its name comes from where it was found – close to the Edmonton rock formation in Alberta (Canada).

It was an **ankylosaur**, one of a group of armoured **herbivores** that lived 76–68 million years ago. There were three main goups of ankylosaurs – ankylosaurids (like Ankylosaurus, see page 118), polacanthids and nodosaurids. Edmontonia was a nodosaurid (see page 128).

Edmontonia was one of the largest nodosaurids at 6–7 m (20–23 ft) in length. It weighed in at around 3,000 kg

(3.5 tons), and its bulky body was supported on four stocky legs. It grew to around 2 m (6 ft) high, and could flatten itself to the ground if attacked to protect its soft underbelly. Even its stiff tail was armoured!

It had **scutes** (bony plates) on its back and head, sharp spikes along its back and tail. Four large spikes stuck out from its shoulders on each side. Small cheek teeth further back in its weak jaws helped it grind up vegetation before swallowing it. The head was probably covered in armoured scales to protect the brain, and two collars of flat bony plates protected the back of the neck – smaller bands of plates continued down to the armoured tail.

MEGA FACTS

- Edmontonia had specially arranged shoulder muscles that let it draw in its front legs if attacked and hold their body close to the ground.

- The large spikes that stuck out from its shoulders were most likely used in contests of strength with others of its own kind.

- Edmontonia had very wide feet, which they would have needed in the mostly low-lying coastal areas they inhabited to walk safely on wet and marshy ground.

- Slow-moving Edmontonia would have needed every bit of its impressive armour, as it shared time and territory with Tyrannosaurus Rex!

Dinosaur Data

PRONUNCIATION:	ED-MON-**TONE**-EE-AH
SUBORDER:	THYREOPHORA
FAMILY:	NODOSAURIDAE
DESCRIPTION:	TANK-LIKE HERBIVORE
FEATURES:	BONY PLATES AND SPIKES FOR PROTECTION
DIET:	LOW-LYING PLANTS

123

SCELIDOSAURUS

Ponderous armoured plant eater

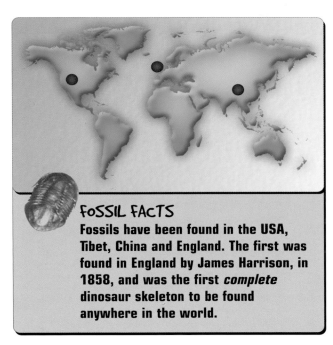

FOSSIL FACTS

Fossils have been found in the USA, Tibet, China and England. The first was found in England by James Harrison, in 1858, and was the first *complete* dinosaur skeleton to be found anywhere in the world.

Scelidosaurus means 'limb lizard'. It was named by Sir Richard Owen in 1859. It lived around 206–200 million years ago.

Scelidosaurus

Appearance

The bony plates in its skin give Scelidosaurus a distinct resemblance to the later **ankylosaurs**. However, the bony plates down its back, and the heavy body raised at the hips also gives it similarities to another later dinosaur, Stegosaurus (see page 116). Scientists believe both **ankylosaurs** and **stegosaurs** may be descended from Scelidosaurus. Its brain was very small compared to its body size, indicating low intelligence.

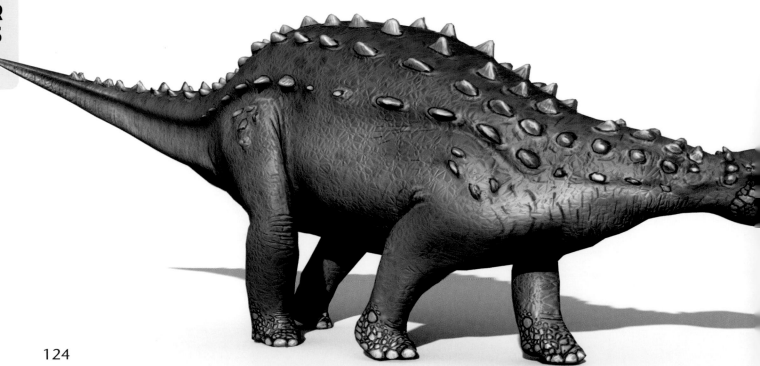

Scelidosaurus harrisonii

Scelidosaurus was a low-slung plant eater, with a small head, stocky legs and a long, stiffened tail. Its neck was quite long compared to other armoured dinosaurs. It weighed some 200–250 kg (440–550 lb) and grew to 1.5 m (5 ft) tall. It was around 4 m (13 ft) long.

It moved slowly, grazing almost constantly on low-growing soft-leaved plants, flowers and fruits. Its narrow beak contained small leaf-shaped teeth in the front of the upper jaw, useful for slicing flowers and fruits off plants rather than for chewing food. It *could* chew, but only with a very simple up and down movement of its jaws.

Defence

The **scutes** that protected it had pointy 'studs' on them, and small three-pronged horns stuck out from behind its ears. If attacked, it would have crouched low to the ground, hiding its soft underbelly and leaving its attacker to fruitlessly bite at its armoured back, flanks and tail.

We know very little for certain about what it ate or where precisely it made its home, as the fossilised remains have

so far all been found away from the creature's natural habitat – the bodies had been washed out to sea after the animal died. They were not marine creatures or amphibians, but probably lived on riverbanks. Perhaps some of them were drowned when the river overflowed, and washed out to sea to be buried and preserved.

MEGA FACTS

- It is thought Scelidosaurus might well have been an ancestor of both Ankylosaurus and Stegosaurus.

- Scelidosaurus has been classified at different times as a stegosaur or an ankylosaur. Scientists still do not wholly agree about which group it belongs to.

- Although it usually walked on all four legs, some scientists think that Scelidosaurus' strong hind legs and long tail may have allowed it to run on just its back legs for short distances.

- Young Scelidosaurus may have added extra protein to their diet by eating insects.

Dinosaur Data

PRONUNCIATION:	SKEL-EE-DOH-**SAWR**-US
SUBORDER:	THYREOPHORA
FAMILY:	SCELIDOSAURIDAE
DESCRIPTION:	ARMOURED HERBIVORE
FEATURES:	BONY ARMOUR PLATES AND SPIKES
DIET:	LOW-GROWING PLANTS

SCUTELLOSAURUS

Tiny armoured herbivore

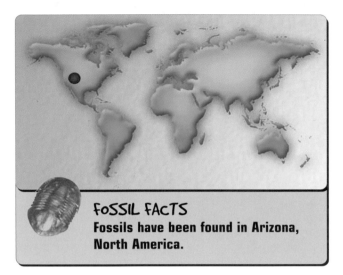

FOSSIL FACTS
Fossils have been found in Arizona, North America.

Scutellosaurus means 'little shield lizard'. It gets its name from the bony armour 'shields' called **scutes** that covered its tiny body. It was named by Edwin Colbert in 1981. We know this little dinosaur from the remains of two incomplete skeletons and hundreds of bony armour plates that have been found in Arizona (USA).

Appearance

Scutellosaurus was a primitive dinosaur. It is the oldest known armoured dinosaur, and is thought to be related to

Lesothaurus. When we think of dinosaurs we tend to think of massive creatures, but Scutellosaurus was no bigger than a dog – 1.2 m (4 ft) long, 1.5 m (5 ft) tall at the hips, and weighing around 10 kg (22 lb). Its long thin tail accounted for much of its length, being twice the length of its combined body and head.

Its thin hind legs were much longer than its forelimbs – scientists believe it probably walked most of the time (and rested) on four legs, but if attacked could rise up onto its back legs and run away at decent speed, its long tail helping to balance it. A creature that can walk on both two and four legs is said to be **semi-bipedal**. Its own ancestors had been fully bipedal – its descendants would be **quadrupeds**.

Scutes

More than 300 bony scutes protected this little creature, running along its back and tail. Six different types of the bony plates have been found. The largest may have formed one or two rows down the centre of its back.

Diet

Scutellosaurus was a **herbivore**, and spent much of its time grazing, using its simple cheek teeth to crush and slice soft and fleshy low-growing vegetation. Its jaw was particularly well-adapted for cropping leafy plants.

Dinosaur Data

PRONUNCIATION:	SKU-**TEL**-OH-**SAWR**-US
SUBORDER:	THYREOPHORA
DESCRIPTION:	TINY ARMOURED HERBIVORE
FEATURES:	LONG THIN TAIL, ARMOURED PLATES
DIET:	PLANTS, SEEDS, FRUITS

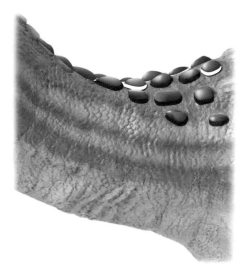

Descendants

Scutellossaurus is most likely an ancestor of the later large armoured **ankylosaurs** (see page 118) and **stegosaurs** (see page 116). Many scientists think that as it developed heavier armoured plates — especially in the head and neck region — its body would have become heavier and heavier at the front, eventually forcing it to walk on all fours permanently and paving the way for its larger quadrupedal descendants.

MEGA FACTS

- Scutellosaurus had two ways to defend itself against attack — it was protected by its armoured skin, and it could rise up onto its back legs to run away.

- Any predator trying to take a bite out of this little guy was in for a shock — its skin was protected by more than 300 armour plates!

- Scutellosaurus had a short skull. Its tail, on the other hand, was twice the length of its body and head put together.

NODOSAURUS

Tank-like armoured herbivore

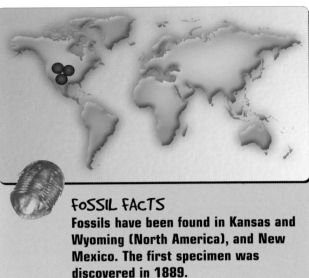

FOSSIL FACTS
Fossils have been found in Kansas and Wyoming (North America), and New Mexico. The first specimen was discovered in 1889.

Appearance

Nodosaurus was 4–6 m (13–20 ft) long and grew up to 3 m (10 ft) high. It moved on four stocky legs, and had five-toed feet. Its front legs were much shorter than its back legs, making its body strongly arched. Its neck was short and its head small.

No Nodosaurus skull has been discovered so its shape has to be deduced from skulls of other nodosaurids. It would probably have had a narrow head, a pointed snout, and powerful jaws with small leaf-shaped teeth back in its cheeks. It may have fed on soft plants. Like other **herbivores**, it may have swallowed small stones (called gastroliths) to aid with grinding up food in its large gut.

Nodosaurus means 'knobbed lizard' or 'node lizard'. It was named by Othniel Charles Marsh in 1889, and takes its name from the bony armour plates and knobs which covered most of its skin. Bony armour plates like those possessed by nodosaurus are called **scutes**. It gave its name to the group of ankylosaurs called **nodosaurids**.

Nodosaurids differ from the other types of ankylosaur in lacking a club at the end of their tail. Nodosaurids were distinguished by the bands of spikes that ran along the sides of their body, pear-shaped heads, and relatively narrow toothless beaks. A bony plate separated their nasal passage from their mouth, so that they could chew food and breathe at the same time.

They had a single large armour plate over the snout, and a solid shield of partially-fused armoured plates protecting the pelvic area. For extra protection, they had bony spikes that stuck out from their flanks.

Nodosaurus attacked by lone raptor

128

Permian period (290-248 million years ago)	**Triassic period** (248-176 million years ago)	**Jurassic period** (176-130 million years ago)	**Cretaceous period** (130-66 million years ago)

Defence

It had armour plating on its back and sides. It had large armoured plates topped with bony nodes on the skin between its ribs, and — unlike other nodosaurids — had dorsal armour, consisting of a pair of midline rectangular scutes with domed centres alternating with bands of smaller, flat and square-shaped scutes. It may have had shoulder or side spikes — remains found so far are not enough to tell us for certain.

Nodosaurus had little means of attacking an enemy. If attacked, it probably relied on crouching low to the ground to protect its soft underside.

MEGA FACTS

- Nodosorous had a small head and minuscule brain compared to the size of its body, indicating very low intelligence.

- In 2003, the fossilised skeleton of an armoured dinosaur that may be a Nodosaurus was found in Kent, England. Except for the missing skull, it is remarkably complete. Only further study will tell us for certain if this is the first Nodosaurus found outside America.

Dinosaur Data

PRONUNCIATION:	NOH-DOH-**SAWR**-US
SUBORDER:	THYREOPHORA
FAMILY:	NODOSAURIDAE
DESCRIPTION:	ARMOURED HERBIVORE

A top view of Nodosaurus's formidable spikes

129

MINMI

Small and unusual armoured herbivore

This dinosaur was named and described by Ralph Molnar in 1980. It was named after the place where the first pieces of its fossil remains had been found, Minmi Crossing.

Minmi was the first armoured dinosaur found south of the equator. It is also the most complete dinosaur skeleton ever found in Australia.

Appearance

Minmi seems to have been a very primitive **ankylosaur** and scientists have found it hard to classify. It has features in common with both ankylosaurs and **nodosaurs**, but is not identical to either. Its snout arched higher than the rest of its skull, which is common in nodosaurs. It had armoured plates like an ankylosaur's – but its legs were longer, and it had no 'club' at the end of its tail.

It would have been about the size of a year-old calf, growing to only 2–3 m (6–10 ft) long and about 1 m (3 ft) high, and weighing around 1,700 kg (3,740 lb). Its back legs were longer than its front ones, and it went on all fours. Minmi would have lived on the low-growing plants of the floodplains and woodlands where it roamed.

As well as having longer legs than ankylosaurus, Minmi had extra bony plates added to its backbone. These strengthened its back, helping support the weight of its armour. Extra muscles attached to these extra plates could have allowed Minmi to run at reasonable speed.

Defence

Minmi had skin armoured with large bony plates (called **scutes**) and smaller pea-sized bones (called **ossicles**) embedded all over it. Even Minmi's underbelly was protected by small bony plates, which makes it unique among the whole thyreophoran suborder of dinosaurs.

Apart from this armour, Minmi had no real way to defend itself – it lacked the tail 'club' possessed by most ankylosaurs. Running away was probably its best defence!

Minmi was the only ankylosaur to have **paravertebrae**. Some scientists have suggested that these are actually **tendons** which have ossified (changed into bone) rather than true bones.

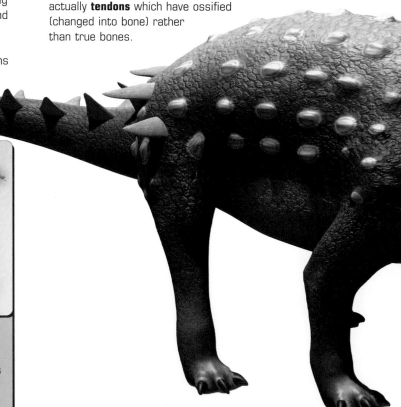

FOSSIL FACTS
Fossils have been found in Queensland, Australia. The first fossils were discovered by Alan Batholomai near Roma, Queensland in 1964.

Minmi skeleton

Minmi has much in common with both ankylosaurs and nodosaurs, but it may turn out to be a wholly new type of armoured dinosaur!

MEGA FACTS

- In 1990 an almost-complete Minmi skeleton was found in Queensland. It was so well preserved that wrinkles in its skin could be made out from the pattern of the ossicles.

- Minmi has the shortest name ever given to a dinosaur.

- Recent studies have been able to analyse the contents of a Minmi stomach. It was able to chew its food into smaller pieces before swallowing them.

Dinosaur Data

PRONUNCIATION:	**MIN**-MEE
SUBORDER:	THYREOPHORA
DESCRIPTION:	SMALL ARMOURED HERBIVORE
FEATURES:	ARMOURED PLATES ON BELLY
DIET:	LOW-GROWING SOFT PANTS MATERIALS, LEAVES, FRUIT, STEMS

PANOPLOSAURUS

Totally armoured reptile

A
R
M
O
U
R
E
D

D
I
N
O
S
A
U
R
S

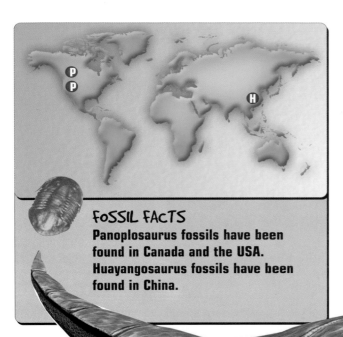

FOSSIL FACTS
Panoplosaurus fossils have been found in Canada and the USA. Huayangosaurus fossils have been found in China.

Dinosaur Data

PRONUNCIATION:	PAN-OH-PLOH-SORE-USS
FAMILY:	ANKYLOSAURIA
DESCRIPTION:	PLANT EATER

Panoplosaurus' skull was wide at the back narrowing to a long toothless snout with a front beak. Much of its skull was protected with a thick bony covering. Its small simple chewing teeth were set into a curving jaw with fleshy cheek pouches for gathering the plants which it ate.

Panoplosaurus was named in 1919.

Thick bony armour covered much of its body with side-facing spikes protruding form its shoulders and forward-facing spokes from its neck. Its low, heavy, stumpy legs would have been covered with thick scaly hide. Panoplosaurus was around 7 m (23 ft) long and weighed up to 4,000 kg (4 tons).

HUAYANGOSAURUS

Huayang reptile

Dinosaur Data

PRONUNCIATION:	HOO-AH-YANG-OH-SORE-USS
FAMILY:	HUAYANGOSAURIDAE
DIET:	PLANT EATER

Dong Zhiming, a famous Chinese **palaeontologist**, named this Huayangosaurus after its place of discovery when it was found in 1982.

The Huayangosaurus belonged to the **stegosaur** family but Huayangosaurus lived in earlier times than its famous relative, the Stegosaurus (see page 116), and was not as widespread. Fossil finds have been restricted to East Asia.

Fossils found show this to have been a small, primitive Stegosaur at around 4 m (13 ft) in height and weighing 400 kg (880 lb). It had pairs of plates all the way down its back and spikes on its tail. Outward-facing spikes above its hips or shoulders would have helped to protect it from attack.

Huayangosaurus skeleton

133

EGGS AND LIFE CYCLE

Eggs

Dinosaurs hatched from eggs laid by females. Dinosaur eggs were a variety of shapes and sizes, and could be up to 60 cm (24 in.) long. Even the biggest dinosaurs had small eggs, because the shell must be thin enough to allow oxygen in and the baby out. These eggs were similar to those of reptiles, birds and primitive mammals; they contained a **membrane** (called the amnion) that kept the embryo moist.

The first fossilised dinosaur eggs found (and the biggest to be found so far) were football-shaped eggs laid by Hypselosaurus (a member of the titanosaurus family, see page 110), found in France in 1869. These eggs were 30 cm (12 in.) long, had a volume of about 2 litres (4 pints) and may have weighed up to 7 kg (15 lb).

Family life

Until recently the only real evidence of dinosaur family life were nests containing eggs from the Gobi Desert,

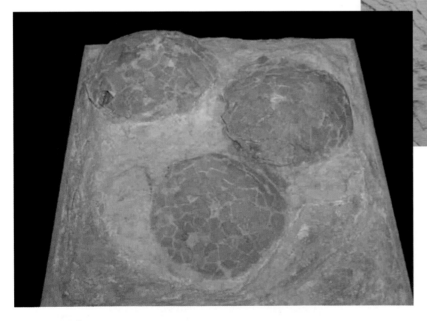

Hypelosaurus egg fossils

Fossilised tracks

discovered in the 1920s and some tracks that showed adults and babies moving together. Very little is known about dinosaur courtship, rivalry, pairing and mating.

More than 200 hundred dinosaur egg sites are now known around the world. The most recent discovery was about ten large dinosaur eggs (plus three egg impressions), found in 1999 in France. Larger egg sites have been found in Spain, where hundreds of thousands of eggs (of both **sauropods** and **theropods**) have been found. Dinosaur eggs sites have also been found in Argentina and China.

Very rarely, the eggs have preserved parts of embryos in them, which can help to match an egg with a species of dinosaur.

Nests, eggs, hatchlings, juveniles and adult Maiasauras (see page 176) were found in one area of the USA. This fossil evidence indicates a high level of parental care and a very social dinosaur.

Some dinosaurs cared for their eggs, others simply laid them and then abandoned them. It is thought that the nesting behaviour of dinosaurs was very similar to the two types that modern birds display – 'precocial' where babies leave the nest as soon as they hatch, and 'altrical', where the helpless young remain in the nest. Dinosaurs also appeared to have some kind of homing instinct, like swallows or pigeons, that guided them back to the same breeding ground year after year.

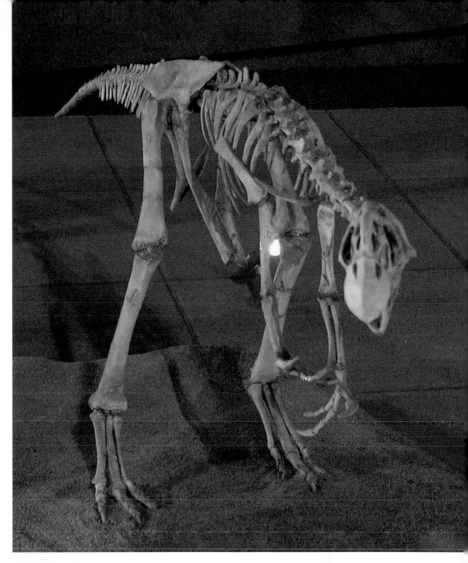

Dinosaur skeleton

Maiasuara eggs

Reproduction

One of the many unanswered questions about dinosaur reproduction is how the giant sauropods (like Apatosaurus (see page 100), Diplodocus (see page 98) and Brachiosaurus (see page 94)) laid their eggs without breaking them. Even if the sauropod squatted while laying eggs, the eggs would be dropped from a height of roughly 2.5 m (8 ft). Some scientists have argued that females may have had a tube that extended from the body for laying eggs (some modern-day turtles have a tube like this).

TRICERATOPS

Gigantic three-horned herbivore

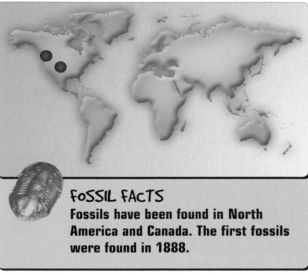

FOSSIL FACTS
Fossils have been found in North America and Canada. The first fossils were found in 1888.

Dinosaur Data

PRONUNCIATION:	TRY-**SER**-A-TOPS
SUBORDER:	MARGINOCEPHALIA (FRINGED HEADS)
FAMILY:	CERATOPSIDAE
DESCRIPTION:	HUGE PLODDING HERBIVORE
FEATURES:	HUGE HEAVY SKULL, THREE HORNS AND BONY NECK FRILL
DIET:	PLANTS AND SHRUBS

The name Triceratops means 'three-horned face' and was chosen because of the creature's most noticeable feature – the three horns on its head. It was fully named *triceratops horridus* ('horrible three-horned face').

Horns and frill

The three horns are striking – one on its snout, and a pair above the eyes about 1 m (3 ft) long. Its other distinctive feature is the bony, stud-surrounded 'frill' at the back of its skull. Scientists have suggested various functions for this frill, but have yet to decide on one. All the following uses have been suggested:

- battling rival Triceratops for status, territory, or food
- display (for communication or attracting mates)
- anchor points for the mighty jaw muscles
- body temperature regulation (by adding to the creature's body surface area and so making absorbing heat, or cooling off, easier)
- protection against **carnivores** biting its neck and front part of body.

Triceratops was a member of the **ceratopsian** dinosaur family – large, horned dinosaurs that lived in herds. They were one of the latest dinosaur families to evolve.

Appearance

Triceratops grew to around 9 m (29 ft) long and 3 m (10 ft) tall, and weighed in at around 5,500 kg (12,100 lb). It had a sharp, parrot-shaped beak that allowed it

MEGA FACTS

- It has been estimated that Triceratops could have run at some 24 km/h (15 mph), even on its short legs – helpful, since it could not take long strides to flee from carnivores such as Tyrannosaurus Rex (see page 54)! Even this didn't always help – several Triceratops skeletons show bite marks that match the teeth of Tyrannosaurus Rex.

- As well as using its sharp beak to slice up vegetation, Triceratops probably also used it in self-defence.

- Triceratops had one of the largest skulls of any land animal so far discovered, sometimes 3 m (10 ft) in length.

- Triceratops is the official state dinosaur of Wyoming and the official state fossil of South Dakota

to break up very tough vegetation, which was then pushed further back into its shearing cheek teeth. It had sturdy short legs and went on all fours. Its head was large, almost a third the length of its barrel-shaped body at 2–3 m (6-9 ft).

Fossilised teeth from Triceratops are among the most commonly found fossils in western North America, and over 50 skulls have been found. Scientists believe it was the dominant herbivore in that area about 72–65 million years ago.

PROTOCERATOPS

Small, hook-beaked herbivore

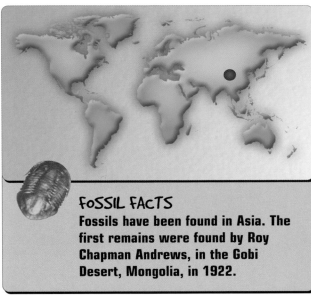

FOSSIL FACTS
Fossils have been found in Asia. The first remains were found by Roy Chapman Andrews, in the Gobi Desert, Mongolia, in 1922.

Protoceratops was small. It grew to about 2 m (6 ft) in length and 75 cm (30 in.) high, but weighed some 400 kg (880 lb). Its skeleton was made of strong, thick bone. It had four short legs, with broad, clawed feet that may have allowed it to run for a short time if threatened. It may even have been able to briefly stand on its hind legs. Most of the time, however, it would have moved slowly and ponderously on all fours.

Its mouth was a strong, curved, parrot-shaped beak, with the upper jaw being longer than the lower. It would have allowed Protoceratops to slice and cut tough plants and vegetation and then push these further back into its jaws, where it could chew them up with the teeth in its cheeks.

Protoceratops means 'first horned face' or 'earliest horned face'. It was named by Walter Granger and W. K. Gregory. It is sometimes also referred to by the shorter name of 'ceratops'.

Appearance

Protoceratops was one of the earliest members of the *ceratopsian* family, and may have been the ancestor of the later horned dinosaurs like Triceratops (see page 136). It lacked well-developed horns and had instead a thick 'bump' of bone on its snout, and small bumps above its eyes – exactly where later horned dinosaurs would have their horns. It also had a large neck frill at the back of its skull.

138

Permian period	Triassic period	Jurassic period	Cretaceous period
(290-248 million years ago)	(248-176 million years ago)	(176-130 million years ago)	(130-65 million years ago)

Skull

The skull of Protoceratops was especially massive, and special muscles were probably attached to its bony neck frill to help it hold up its heavy head. The skull of a Protoceratops made up nearly half of its whole body length!

Dinosaur Data

PRONUNCIATION:	PRO-TOE-**SERR**-A-TOPS
SUBORDER:	MARGINOCEPHALIA
FAMILY:	PROTOCERATOPSIDAE
DESCRIPTION:	SMALL, HEAVY, HUGE-SKULLED HERBIVORE
FEATURES:	MASSIVE SKULL, NECK FRILL
DIET:	TOUGH PLANTS AND VEGETATION

Frill

Its broad, bony neck frill grew as the Protoceratops aged. Scientists have suggested various functions for this frill – to protect the neck, to impress other Protoceratops, or to anchor jaw muscles. Some believe it may have been brightly coloured to help the Protoceratops attract a mate or to intimidate enemies.

Protoceratops probably lived in herds.

MEGA FACTS

- A robotic protoceratops has been created at the Massachusetts Institute of Technology.

- In 1971, the fossil remains of a Velociraptor locked in combat with a Protoceratops were found in Mongolia (see page 67).

139

ARRHINOCERATOPS

No nose-horn face

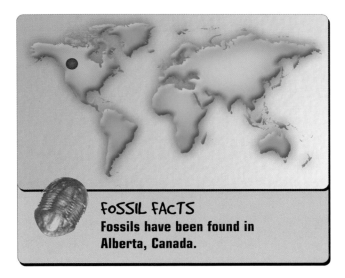

FOSSIL FACTS
Fossils have been found in Alberta, Canada.

W.A. Parks gave it the name meaning 'no nose-horn face' as the fossilised skull appeared to have a bumpy lump, unlike Anchiceratops or Triceratops (see page 136), which had a horn there. However, later investigations show that, in common with other **ceratopsians** the Arrhinoceratops did have a true horn on its nose.

Appearance

Arrhinoceratops stood a massive 6 m (20 ft) off the ground – a similar size to its close relative Triceratops (see page 136). With its outward-pointing horns and large neck frill it would have looked even bigger. It weighed 35,000 kg (3.5 tons).

The frill around its neck, as well as making it look bigger and more impressive, would have frightened off predators and made them attractive to potential mates. Both male and female Arrhinoceratops had large neck frills. Although their head, horn and neck frills were similar in size to those of Triceratops, they had hollow areas in the supporting bone. This would make them slightly lighter although they still needed very strong neck muscles to support the weight. The two horns at either side of its head are believed to have been outward-facing rather than forward-facing but **palaeontologists** have found it quite difficult to tell from the fossils which have been discovered.

Defence and diet

If attacked, Arrhinoceratops could defend itself by giving a sharp peck to its attacker with its fierce parrot-like beak. They did not use their teeth in doing this as they were

Permian period	Triassic period	Jurassic period	Cretaceous period
(290-248 million years ago)	(248-176 million years ago)	(176-130 million years ago)	(130-66 million years ago)

located deeper inside its mouth high up in its cheeks. Its beak was also used for pecking and cutting leaves and needles off plants and trees for food. There were few flowering plants around at the time so Arrhinoceratops would have lived mainly on a diet of ferns, cycads and pine needles.

Arrhinoceratops are believed to have lived and travelled around in herds feeding off vegetation as they moved. Palaentologists believe this because groups of fossils have been found together. It may be that they died in one place but it may be that many corpses gathered over a wide area over time and then their skeletons got washed away together in storms so that they were fossilised together.

Dinosaur Data

PRONUNCIATION:	AY-RYE-NO-SERRA-TOPS
FAMILY:	CERATOPSIDAE
DESCRIPTION:	HORNED PLANT EATER
FEATURES:	NECK FRILL AND HORNS
DIET:	PLANTS

MEGA FACTS

- Arrhinoceratops belong to the ceratopsian group which was the last group of dinosaurs to evolve. Despite having had a long time to evolve as a group it seems that they changed very little over the course of time.

- The neck frill had holes in the bone which are called *fenestrae* (windows). This made the bone lighter so that its head was not impossibly heavy to hold up.

- Arrhinoceratops was about the same size a rhinoceros.

141

MICROCERATOPS

Tiny bipedal herbivore

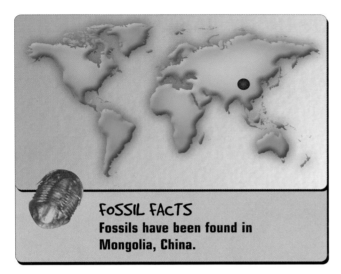

fOSSIL FACTS
Fossils have been found in Mongolia, China.

Microceratops means 'tiny horned face'. It was named in 1953 and is the smallest known horned dinosaur.

This tiny, slender herbivore lived in Asia, around 80 million years ago. It was a **cerotopsian** and became extinct at the end of the Cretaceous period.

Appearance

Small and slim, Microceratops was almost fragile-looking, with a small body and slender limbs. It was closely related to the larger Protoceratops (see page 138) and looked a lot like its bigger relative.

It grew to a mere 76 cm (30 in.) long and 60 cm (24 in.) high. This was a dinosaur you could have picked up in one hand.

Its head was around 20 cm (8 in.) long, and it had a horny parrot-like beak. A small bony neck frill jutted from the back of its skull. Despite its name, it lacked any real horns. Scientists have suggested various functions for the neck frill (all the ceratopsian dinosaurs had one) – it might have been to protect the neck, to impress other Microceratops, or to anchor jaw muscles.

Some scientists believe the neck frill may have been brightly coloured, to help the dinosaur attract a mate or to intimidate enemies. It seems unlikely that little Microceratops did much intimidating. Running away would be its best defence.

Its limbs were particularly slender compared to those of other dinosaurs. Its hind legs were longer than its front ones, and scientists believe it would have been able to stand up on its hind legs to run and move around (it would have been **bipedal**) though it may have gone down on all fours to graze and browse for food.

The lower part of its hind legs was much longer than the upper part, suggesting Microceratops would have been a swift runner. The front legs, or 'arms', really were tiny in comparison – a bone from the upper part of a Microceratops front limb was only 10 cm (4 in.) long.

Permian period	Triassic period	Jurassic period	Cretaceous period
(290-248 million years ago)	(248-176 million years ago)	(176-130 million years ago)	(130-66 million years ago)

Diet

Microceratops was an herbivore that spent much of its time eating. It fed on **ferns**, **cycads** and **conifers**, using its sharp parrot-like beak to bite off leaves and needles. These would then be pushed back further into its mouth where cheek teeth could grind up the food before it was swallowed.

Microceratops probably lived in herds, grazing from place to place. It laid eggs, and the herd most likely shared one big nesting area, as a defence against larger predators.

MEGA FACTS

- Microceratops appeared as part of the herd in the Walt Disney film *Dinosaur* (2000).

- Microceratops was not quite the smallest dinosaur that ever lived — that was *Compsognathus Longpipes*, which was only the size of a chicken.

Dinosaur Data

PRONUNCIATION:	MY-KRO-**SAYR**-AH-TOPS
SUBORDER:	MARGINOCEPHALIA
FAMILY:	PROTOCERATOPSIDAE
DESCRIPTION:	TINY FRILLED HERBIVORE
FEATURES:	SMALL SIZE, LONG HIND LEGS, FRILL
DIET:	FERNS, CYCADS, CONIFERS

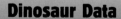

LEPTOCERATOPS

Small and swift parrot-beaked herbivore

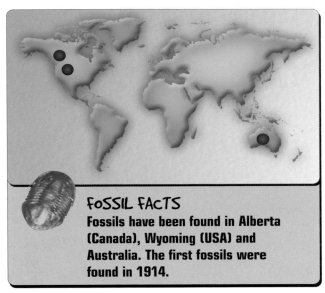

FOSSIL FACTS
Fossils have been found in Alberta (Canada), Wyoming (USA) and Australia. The first fossils were found in 1914.

This small, agile **ceratopsian** dinosaur was described in 1914, and named by Barnum Brown in the same year. No complete skeleton for it has been discovered – we know it from five skulls and varied skeletal remains.

Appearance

A recent study has suggested that Leptoceratops had an extended beak taking up much of its face. Leptoceratops had only a very few teeth, further back in its jaws, which are different to those of other ceratopsians in that instead of having double roots, its teeth had a single root per tooth. This may have meant they were less firmly anchored in its jaw – a potential problem when feeding on tough vegetation. It could use its sharp, parrot-shaped beak to slice off leaves, or needles, and to break open fruits and seeds.

Leptoceratops lacked horns, but did have a neck frill where the bones at the back of its skull formed a peak – this frill was small and flat, but distinctive.

Leptoceratops is believed to have been one of the fastest ceratopsians – perhaps even *the* fastest.

Leptoceratops grew to around 2.4 m (8 ft) long. Scientists believe it may have spent most of its time walking or standing on its back legs. Its forelimbs had five-fingered hands with claws that could be used for grasping vegetation. It would still have been capable of moving on all fours. Some scientists even think it may have used its powerful back legs to dig burrows in which to hide from predators.

In 1999, remains from six different Leptoceratops were found close together in a **bonebed**, suggesting that perhaps they spent at least some time in social groups.

MEGA FACTS

- Leptoceratops was, until very recently, believed to have lived only in North America and Canada, where almost all fossil remains of it have been found. More recently, fossilised Leptoceratops bones have been found in Australia, showing that this primitive herbivore may have lived all over the world.

- The fossil finds in Australia also date from the early Cretaceous period, whereas all previous finds dated from toward the end of that period. It seems Leptoceratops may have walked the Earth for some 50 million years!

- Leptoceratops' teeth were different to those of its fellow ceratopsians. They were broad instead of long, which may have helped it chew up all kinds of different vegetation. Each tooth had only one replacement tooth available — most ceratopsians had several teeth ready to take the place of one that was broken or fell out.

Dinosaur Data

PRONUNCIATION:	LEP-TOE-**SERR**-A-TOPS
SUBORDER:	MARGINOCEPHALIA
FAMILY:	PROTOCERATOPIDAE
DESCRIPTION:	SMALL AND AGILE HERBIVORE
FEATURES:	SMALL, FLAT NECK FRILL, PARROT-SHAPED BEAK
DIET:	LOW-LYING PLANTS

STYGIMOLOCH

Fearsome-looking herbivore

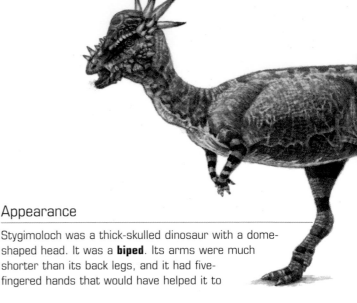

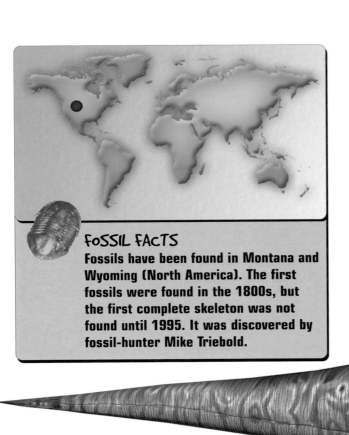

FOSSIL FACTS

Fossils have been found in Montana and Wyoming (North America). The first fossils were found in the 1800s, but the first complete skeleton was not found until 1995. It was discovered by fossil-hunter Mike Triebold.

Appearance

Stygimoloch was a thick-skulled dinosaur with a dome-shaped head. It was a **biped**. Its arms were much shorter than its back legs, and it had five-fingered hands that would have helped it to

Stygimoloch means 'demon from the River Styx' or 'river devil'. In Greek myth, the River Styx flowed through the underworld called Hades (Hell).

The remains were found in a rock formation named 'Hell Creek', so the dinosaur was named for the 'hell river'. Moloch was a fearsome Semitic god or demon – the ring of horns on Stygimoloch's head gave it, its finders thought, a demonic appearance.

grasp vegetation. Stygimoloch was a **herbivore**. It grazed the woodlands of North America 74–65 million years ago.

Its round head was covered in bony spikes and bumps, and it had a whole collection

of horns, some as long as 10 cm (4 in.). It was a small dinosaur, growing no more than 2–3 m (7–10 ft) long and most likely weighing no more than 100 kg (220 lb). It would have stood 1.2 m (4 ft) high.

The 1995 discovery of a complete Stygimoloch skeleton, and study of it, cast doubt on the long-held belief that Stygimoloch butted heads with one another like goats to battle for females or status within the herd.

The new find suggested that if Stygimoloch had tried something like this, it would probably have broken its neck! Some scientists do still believe they may have headbutted other dinosaurs on their vulnerable underbellies, though. Others believe the spikes simply served to identify Stygimoloch to others of its kind.

MEGA FACTS

- The first appearance of Stygimoloch in a film was in the Disney movie *Dinosaur* in 2000.

- It probably lived in herds.

- In 2003, Clayton Phipps found the world's only complete Stygimoloch skull. Its value is estimated at $150,000–$1million. Many scientists are opposed to the sale and auction of fossils, as it often results in specimens passing into private collections rather than public museums where they can be properly studied.

- The teeth in the back of its mouth resembled those of Stegosaurus, but the front of its mouth was full of sharp incisors, very like those of a carnivore.

Dinosaur Data

PRONUNCIATION:	**STIG**-IH-**MOE**-LOCK
SUBORDER:	CERAPODA
FAMILY:	PACHYCEPHALOSAURIA
DESCRIPTION:	SMALL, SPIKY HERBIVORE
FEATURES:	DOME-SHAPED HEAD, HORNS AND SPIKES
DIET:	LEAVES AND PLANTS

CENTROSAURUS

Horned herbivore

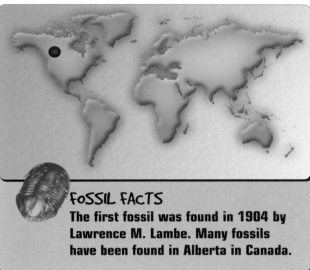

FOSSIL FACTS
The first fossil was found in 1904 by Lawrence M. Lambe. Many fossils have been found in Alberta in Canada.

Dinosaur Data

PRONUNCIATION:	**SEN**-TRO-SAWR-US
SUBORDER:	MARGINOCEPHALIA
FAMILY:	CERATOPSIDAE
DESCRIPTION:	LARGE HORNED HERBIVORE
FEATURES:	SINGLE LARGE HORN ON ITS NOSE, BONY FRILL RISING BACK FROM THE TOP OF ITS SKULL
DIET:	LOW-LYING PLANTS

Centrosaurus means 'sharp pointed lizard' and comes from the Greek words *kentron* (sharp point) and *sauros* (lizard). It was named by Lawrence Lamb for the distinctive large pointed horn growing from its nose.

Centrosaurus was about 6 m (20 ft) long, 1.8 m (6 ft) tall and weighed about 3,000 kg (3 tons). It had four short powerful legs that ended in feet with five toes. Each toe had a short claw and the foot had developed hoofed pads.

Centrosaurus walked on all fours and grazed on low-lying vegetation that it could reach with its powerful beak. It used its beak to tear off vegetation that it then pushed further back into its mouth to be chewed by rows of cheek teeth.

Its most distinctive features were the impressive horn growing from its nose and the scalloped bony frill that swept up from its skull. The nasal horn was 46 cm (18 in.) long! In different species of Centrosaurus this horn curved either forward or backward. Its bony frill was scalloped, meaning it had a wavy edge, and the tips of the frill each bore a small spiky horn. Unlike Triceratops (see page 136), Centrosaurus had only very short horns (little more than bumps) above its eyes but

| Permian period
(290-248 million years ago) | Triassic period
(248-176 million years ago) | Jurassic period
(176-130 million years ago) | |

MEGA FACTS

- Scientists think that if the herd was threatened the males would form a circle, facing outwards with their fierce horns to protect the females and young.

- A fragmentary fossil of a creature very similar to Centrosaurus was found by Edward Drinker Cope in 1876 and named 'Monoclonius'. Some scientists believe this was actually the first find of a Centrosaurus. If this is proven then the name will change to the one given by the first discoverer – so Centrosaurus would be known as Monoclonius!

- Centrosaurus was the first of the 'short-frilled' ceratops to be discovered.

- A new species of Centrosaurus (Centrosaurus Brinkmani) was discovered by Dr Michael Ryan and Dr Tony Russell in 2005. It was named after Dr Don Brinkman, another palaeontologist.

it did have two prominent horns that curved forward from the middle of its frill. These horns were much longer than those on the rest of the frill.

Many fossil finds of Centrosaurus have been made in Red Deer River valley in Alberta, Canada. Here **palaeontologists** have found vast **bonebeds** containing the fossils of thousands of Centrosaurus specimens. The fact that so many were found in the same place strongly suggests that Centrosaurus was a social animal, travelling in large herds to find the best sources of food.

Spectacular horned herbivore

FOSSIL FACTS
Fossils have been found In Alberta (Canada) and Montana (USA). The first remains were found in Alberta (Canada) in 1913, by palaeontologist Lawrence M. Lambe.

Styracosaurus means 'spiked lizard'. It had the most impressive set of horns ever seen in the animal kingdom – six long horns stuck out backwards from its neck frill, it had a smaller horn above each eye, and a single horn 60 cm (2 ft) long and 15 cm (6 in.) wide protruded from its nose!

Appearance

Some 5.5 m (18 ft) in length and 2 m (6 ft) tall, Styracosaurus was about the size of an elephant and, like an elephant, its skin was tough and thick, making it a far from easy target for predators. It had a large, bulky body and could weigh up to 3,000 kg (3 tons). Its four sturdy legs were

short and strong, and Styracosaurus went on all fours. Unlike earlier frilled and horned dinosaurs, Styracosaurus' four-toed feet had blunt hooves instead of claw-like ones. It had a massive head and a short, pointed tail.

It had a powerful, hooked beak, with teeth further back in the side of its jaws, designed to let it tear and chew up the tough leaves of the low-growing plants on which it lived. Like other **ceratopsian** dinosaurs, it had large nasal openings in its deep snout – no one has yet discovered why this was useful to these creatures.

Styracosaurus probably lived in herds, moving around their territory and feeding grounds slowly in large groups, and taking care of their young once they hatched. Large deposits of its fossilised bones (one contained some 100 Styracosaurus fossils!) have been found together in one area.

MEGA FACTS

- Styracosaurus was an ancestor of Triceratops (see page 136).

- In spite of its bulk, scientists believe Styracosaurus might have been able to run at up to 32 km/h (20 mph) when it needed to! That's just a little faster than car is allowed to go on the street where you live.

- A Styracosaurus was seen on film in 1969, badly miscast as a fearsome predator in *The valley of Gwangi*. In 2000, it played a more peaceful role in the Walt Disney film *Dinosaur*.

- In May 2006, Styracosaurus took up residence in the toy section of the famous department store *Harrods*. Working full-time for seven weeks, two builders created a remarkable 375 kg (825 lb) LEGO model of the spiky dinosaur, using 180,000 LEGO bricks! It took them an incredible 506 hours to build, and the model is not only spectacular to see but can roar at passers-by from its setting of palm trees and tropical background noises.

Dinosaur Data

PRONUNCIATION:	STY-RACK-OH-**SAWR**-US
SUBORDER:	MARGINOCEPHALIA
FAMILY:	CERATOPSIDAE
DESCRIPTION:	HORNED AND FRILLED HERBIVORE
FEATURES:	SPECTACULAR HORNS, NECK FRILL, BEAK
DIET:	LOW-LYING PLANTS

PSITTACOSAURUS

Small parrot-beaked herbivore

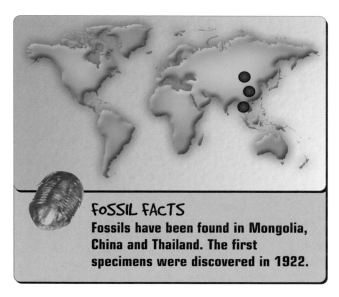

FOSSIL FACTS
Fossils have been found in Mongolia, China and Thailand. The first specimens were discovered in 1922.

on the nose, and all had short bony spikes sticking out backward from the sides of the head. Its rather square skull was small and narrow, with eyes and nostrils placed high on the sides of the head. A pair of hornlike bumps could be seen on the sides of its skull.

It had a hook-like beak, with a very few spade-shaped teeth further back in the jaw. This would have helped it to slice and crop the new, tougher types of plants that were appearing and help it to break open fruits and seeds.

Appearance

Psittacosaurus was just over a metre tall and perhaps 2 m (6 ft) long from the tip of its parrot-like beak to the end of its long, counter-balancing tail. It made up for lack of size with speed and strength. Most of the time it was **bipedal**, standing on its two strong hind legs. Its front legs – or arms – were much shorter and were probably mostly used

Psittacosaurus means 'parrot lizard'. The name comes from this primitive dinosaur's distinctly parrot-shaped beak. (*Psittacus* is the Latin word for parrot). It was a very primitive horned dinosaur that lived 110 million years ago.

Some scientists consider Psittacosaurus to be a likely ancestor of the later horned dinosaurs like Triceratops (see page 136). Some had a small horn

Dinosaur Data

PRONUNCIATION:	**SIT**-AH-KOE-**SAWR**-US
SUBORDER:	MARGINOCEPHALIA
FAMILY:	PSITTACOSAURIDAE
DESCRIPTION:	SMALL, AGILE HERBIVORE
FEATURES:	PARROT-SHAPED BEAK, BOXY SKULL
DIET:	TOUGH PLANTS, FRUITS AND SEEDS

Permian period	Triassic period	Jurassic period	Cretaceous period
(290-248 million years ago)	(248-176 million years ago)	(176-130 million years ago)	(130-66 million years ago)

for grasping vegetation. There were four long fingers on each hand. Its massive descendants, like Triceratops, had to go on four legs all the time, especially as their massive skulls put a lot of weight at the front end of their bodies.

This small, agile herbivore may have lived in herds, like most **ceratopsians**.

MEGA FACTS

- A Psittacosaurus weighed no more than 25–80 kg (55–176 lb).

- Scientists have studied growth lines in Psittacosaurus bones (much as one might count tree rings to work out the age of a tree) and estimate it would have had a lifespan of at least 10 years.

- It is assumed that its best defence was to run away fast on its powerful hind legs.

- Some Psittacosaurus fossils have preserved the impressions of skin – its hide was covered with fine, pebble-like scales, with larger scales (called scutes) over its shoulder area.

- One of the smallest dinosaurs fossils ever discovered is that of a baby Psittacosaurus less than 40 cm (16 in.) long. New hatchlings would have been even smaller.

Psittacosaurus was between 1 and 2 m high

Psittacosaurus skeleton

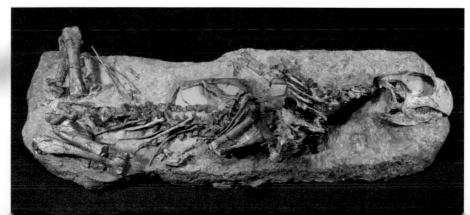

153

SKELETONS

Study of all dinosaurs starts with the skeletons. We have discovered several well-preserved skeletons to identify.

Anatomically, dinosaurs have skeletal features that distinguish them from other **archosaurs** (crocodilians and **pterosaurs** (see page 199). Dinosaurs have reduced fourth and fifth digits (like fingers) on their hands, their feet have three large toes, they have three or more vertebrae making up the sacrum (fused vertebrae by the hip), and have an open hip socket (a three-bone structure).

This hip structure gives dinosaurs a posture that positions their legs under their bodies, unlike other reptiles, which have legs that sprawl out to the sides. Dinosaurs were the first to be able to walk with straight legs tucked underneath their bodies. It has never been achieved by any other reptile before, or since, and it opened the way to the evolution of a variety of body types and lifestyles. This helped them to become the dominant land animals for 160 million years.

Classification

Dinosaurs are classified by their hip structure, into the order saurischia (meaning lizard-hipped) and the order ornithischia (meaning bird-hipped). This division is based on their evolutionary tree; early in the Triassic period, dinosaurs branched into these two groups from their ancestors, the **thecodonts**.

Skulls

The dinosaurs were diapsids (as are all reptiles except turtles), which are animals that had two extra holes in the sides of their skulls.

Dinosaur skeletons differed from species to species. Utahraptor, (a member of the **therapod** family), was a swift and terrifying predator that stood taller than a man. Its skeleton was lightly built, making it swift and able to move about easily, while its long tail helped it to balance. This allowed it to perform acrobatic feats, such as jumping and balancing on one foot.

Hypsilophodon

Hypsilophodon

Hypsilophodon (see page 165) was a two-legged plant eater standing just 1.5 m (5 ft) high. The most striking feature about a Hypsilophodon skeleton is how little there is of it. Rather like a gazelle or antelope, the whole structure had been slimmed down to give maximum support for minimum weight. Even the bones were thin-walled and hollow, just like a gazelle's. A Hypsilophodon's thigh bone was quite short, allowing it to be pulled rapidly back and forth for fast strides.

Tyrannosaurus Rex

Giant meat eater Tyrannosaurus Rex had a bulky body, a big head with powerful jaws, sharp teeth, and a stiff tail. Its front legs were tiny. It probably had about 200 bones, roughly the same as a human (no one knows exactly how many it had, since no complete Tyrannosaurus skeletons have been found). Scientists cannot agree whether Tyrannosaurus was capable of fast movement or not. Its skeleton is heavy and does not suggest a fast mover, but the upper foot bones are locked together for strength, possibly to withstand the stresses of running, indicating that perhaps it was a fast-moving animal.

Dinosaur skull showing two extra holes in sides of skull

Complete mounted dinosaur skeleton from the Natural History Museum, London

IGUANODON

Thumb-spiked herbivore

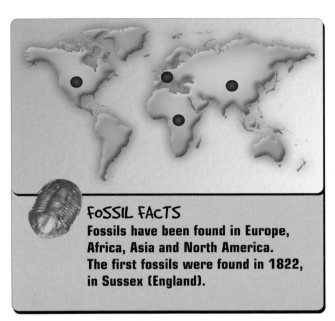

FOSSIL FACTS
Fossils have been found in Europe, Africa, Asia and North America. The first fossils were found in 1822, in Sussex (England).

Dinosaur Data

PRONUNCIATION:	IG-**WAN**-OH-**DON**
SUBORDER:	ORNITHOPODA
FAMILY:	IGUANODONTIDAE
DESCRIPTION:	SUCCESSFUL HERBIVORE
FEATURES:	HIGHLY-SPECIALISED HANDS, PARROT-LIKE BEAK
DIET:	CYCADS, CONIFER LEAVES, FERNS, HORSETAILS

Iguanodon means 'iguana tooth'. It was named in 1825. Some of the first Iguanodon remains found were teeth, and they were very like those of the lizard Iguana – except the dinosaur teeth were twenty times bigger!

Iguanodon was the second dinosaur ever to be named. (Megalosaurus was first – see page 80.)

Appearance

Iguanodon had a bulky body, a stiff, flat tail, and a snout ending in a horny beak. It grew up to 10 m (33 ft) long, 5 m (16 ft) tall and stood 2.78 m (9 ft) high at the hip. It weighed up to 5,000 kg (5 tons).

There were no teeth in its horny beak but it did have cheek teeth further back, about 5 cm (2 in.) long.

It would use its beak to nip vegetation from trees and plants, then push its food further back into its mouth to be ground up by the teeth. Iguanodon was unusual because it could actually chew its food. Most reptiles cannot do this. Iguanodon's specially-hinged upper jaw could flex from side to side, so its upper teeth ground over the lower ones.

Iguanodon had highly unusual forepaws. They could be used as hands for grasping, and also as feet for walking. The middle three fingers were linked together with webbing or padding (scientists are not sure which). The little finger was not linked to any other, and could curl and grasp things. Most unusual was the thumb – it was a sharp spike between 5 and 15 cm (2 and 6 in.) long. The purpose of this spike is still unclear – it may have been used for picking up and holding food, or (more likely) in self-defence.

Fossil footprints exist that showing Iguanodon walking on all fours. But some scientists think it only grazed on four legs, and did most of its moving on just its hind legs. It had sturdy, pillar-like back legs, which were much longer than its slender front ones. The back feet had only three toes. Scientists agree that it could rear to get food, or run away. It may have been capable of running at speeds up to 15–20 km/h (9–12 mph)!

Bonebed discoveries where dozens of Iguanodon skeletons were found together show it was an animal that lived in herds.

MEGA FACTS

- Iguanodon's razor-sharp thumb spike was at first thought to belong on its nose, as a kind of horn.

- Iguanodon bones have been found on nearly every continent of the world.

- An Iguanodon appears on the Coat of Arms of Maidstone, an English town close to where its fossils were found.

An Iguanadon footprint

GALLIMIMUS

Fast-moving bird-like dinosaur

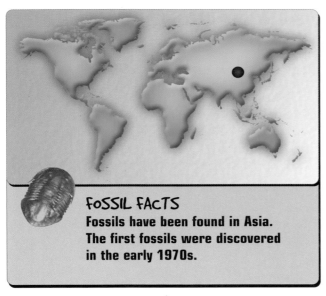

FOSSIL FACTS
**Fossils have been found in Asia.
The first fossils were discovered
in the early 1970s.**

Gallimimus means 'chicken mimic' or 'rooster mimic'. It was named in 1972, for its resemblance to a huge bird.

Appearance

It grew to a length of between 4 and 6 m (13 and 20 ft). It had a long neck, round head and prominent long, thin and flat toothless beak. The bottom front part of its beak had a distinctive 'shovel' shape. Its brain was comparatively large in relation to its body weight, making it one of the most intelligent of the dinosaurs. Its eyes were set on either side of its head, making depth perception impossible.

Gallimimus had hollow bones, but even so weighed some 400–500 kg (88–1,100 lb). It had a long tail that would help to stabilise it as it ran on its strong back legs.

Diet

Gallimimus was closely related to **carnivorous** predators like Tyrannosaurus Rex (see page 54). It was thought until recently that it too probably preyed on small animals (like lizards) and used its beak to break open the eggs of other dinosaurs. In 2001, a fossil specimen was found showing that Gallimimus had peculiar tiny comb-like structures in its mouth. This plate strongly resembled the one a modern duck uses to 'filter feed' – to filter out food particles from water.

This changed the way we think about Gallimimus' diet. Because fossils showed it to have weak jaw muscles, scientists supposed it ate stolen eggs or chased down weak prey. It is now believed Gallimimus may not have used its beak to kill prey at all.

MEGA FACTS

- Gallimimus could probably run up to 70 km/h (43 mph)! That would make it the fastest dinosaur that ever lived.

- Unlike earlier 'ostrich dinosaurs', Gallimimus had no teeth at all.

- We do not know for sure if it lived in herds or was a solitary creature.

It probably fed by straining food (tiny **invertebrates**, insects and plant material) out of water and sediment from the bottom of ponds and rivers. No one had expected to find evidence of filter-feeding in such large, land-based dinosaur!

Gallimimus being a filter-feeder would make sense because its fossils have been found in rocks that would have been wet environments when it lived. It would also explain why the lower front part of its beak possesses a distinctive 'shovel' shape.

Dinosaur Data

PRONUNCIATION:	**GALL**-IH-**MIME**-US
SUBORDER:	THEROPODA
FAMILY:	ORNITHOMIMIDAE
DESCRIPTION:	OSTRICH-LIKE **OMNIVORE**
FEATURES:	LONG LEGS, SMALL HEAD, FLEXIBLE NECK, PROMINENT BEAK
DIET:	MAY HAVE EATEN INSECTS, LIZARDS, EGGS, PLANTS OR STRAINED FOOD PARTICLES FROM WATER AND MUD

DRINKER

Small bipedal herbivore

FOSSIL FACTS
Drinker fossils have been found in the USA.

Dinosaur Data

PRONUNCIATION:	**DRINK**-ER
SUBORDER:	ORNITHOPODA
FAMILY:	HYPSILOPHODONTIDAE
DESCRIPTION:	SMALL BIPEDAL HERBIVORE
FEATURES:	FLEXIBLE TAIL
DIET:	SWAMP VEGETATION AND PLANTS

Drinker is named in honour of the scientist and dinosaur expert Edward Drinker Cope, who lived between 1840 and 1897.

Three partial skeletons of Drinker have been found. They are an adult, a youngster (or 'sub adult') and a child ('juvenile') so we can see what the dinosaur looked like at various stages of its life.

Drinker was quite a small dinosaur, growing to around 2 m (6 ft) long and 1 m (3 ft) high. It weighed only 25 kg (55 lb). Drinker was **bipedal**, had a flexible tail, and ate plants.

Drinker remains were found near those of marsh vegetation and lungfish teeth — so we think it lived near the swampy shores of lakes. Scurrying through swamps and forest undergrowth may have helped this little dinosaur hide from terrifying predators like Allosaurus (see page 72).

Drinker

Edward Drinker Cope and the great bone wars

Cope poured his wealth into the search for dinosaur discoveries. His great rival was another famous **palaeontologist** called Othniel Charles Marsh. The two men started out as friends, but in 1868 Cope discovered that Marsh had bribed the owners of a quarry which often sent dinosaur bones to Cope to send them to him (Marsh) instead. Thus was born a feud and rivalry between the two that would last almost 30 years and become known as 'the Bone Wars'.

Edward Drinker Cope (1840 – 97)

MEGA FACTS

- Drinker might have lived in burrows close to marshes. Drinker had a flexible tail, unlike those of many dinosaurs, which would have allowed it to curl up in a burrow.

- Drinker had large feet, that helped it to move quickly and quietly.

The feud was worsened when Marsh pointed out that Cope had placed the head of his re-assembled Elasmosaurus (see page 36) on the end of the skeleton's tail rather than its neck. Marsh made sure this mistake got plenty of publicity. The next year, Cope retaliated by luring away one of Marsh's assistants, and having his people start digging in one of Marsh's excavations in Kansas.

The feud became a competition between the two, to see who could discover more new species of dinosaur, and collect more fossil remains. The two scientists did very little excavation work themselves – they paid other collectors to do it for them. Cope once stole an entire train full of Marsh's fossils, and Marsh blew up one of his sites with dynamite rather than let Cope work there.

'The Bone Wars' lasted right up to the death of Cope in 1897. When Cope and Marsh began their work, only 18 dinosaur species were known in America – between them they raised this number to over 150.

Othniel C. Marsh (1831 – 99)

161

LEAELLYNASAURA

Sharp-eyed Antarctic herbivore

BIRD-FOOTED DINOSAURS

FOSSIL FACTS
Fossils have been found in Australia. The first fossils were discovered in 1989.

Dinosaur Data

PRONUNCIATION:	LEE-ELL-LIN-AH-**SAWR**-AH
SUBORDER:	ORNITHOPODA
FAMILY:	HYPSILOPHODONTIDAE
DESCRIPTION:	SMALL BIPEDAL HERBIVORE
FEATURES:	HUGE EYES, BIG BRAIN, LONG HIND LEGS
DIET:	FERNS, MOSSES, HORSETAILS, LEAVES

Leaellynasaura means 'Leaellyn's lizard'. It was named in 1989. Like Maiasaura (see page 176), it has the feminine Greek name-ending -*saura* rather than -*saurus*.

This little **herbivore** was discovered first in Australia. In the late Cretaceous period, the continents were very different to the ones we recognise today. This part of Australia would have been well inside the Antarctic Circle, almost at the South Pole!

No reptile could live there today, but Leaellynasaura seemed to thrive there. Although the area was forested then, and days would have been fairly warm, the nights would have been long and cold. Leaellynasaura would have had to live without the sun for weeks or even months at a time!

Scientists believe Leaellynasaura lived in herds, and could have huddled together for warmth. That it could survive in the Antarctic cold and dark has even made some scientists think Leaellynsaura may have been warm-blooded.

Appearance

An adult Leaellynasaura would have been about 2.5 m (8 ft) long, and only 50 cm (18 in.) tall at the hip. It weighed about 10 kg (22 lb). It stood on its hind legs (was **bipedal)** and had a long tail. Its hind legs were long and strong, as were its hind feet. Its front legs (its arms) were much shorter, and ended in hands.

Leallynasaura's 17 cm (7 in.) long skull shows that this dinosaur had very large eyes. The skull also has unusually large holes where the optic nerves connected back to the brain.

Scientists think Leaellynasaura must have had very good eyesight, and developed the ability to see in the dark thanks to living through dark Antarctic winters.

Diet

Leaellynasaura had a tough horned beak. It probably fed on **horsetails**, mosses and **ferns** which grew on the floor of the Antarctic forests. **Conifers** and **ginko** would have grown in the forests where it lived. It may even have scrambled up into trees to reach leaves. It would have used its beak to rip off leaves, then pushed them further back into its mouth, to be ground up by the cheek teeth in its strong jaws.

MEGA FACTS

- We know from its skull that Leaellynasaura had a large brain compared to the size of its body — it was one smart dinosaur.

- Some scientists think Leaellynasaura survived the dark winter days by hibernating, like tortoises.

- Leaellynasaura built nests on the ground to lay their eggs in. A hatchling would have been only 30 cm (12 in.) long.

Leaellynasaura

CAMPTOSAURUS

Flexible reptile

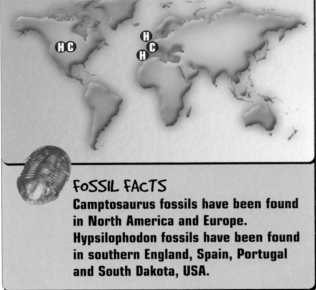

FOSSIL FACTS
Camptosaurus fossils have been found in North America and Europe. Hypsilophodon fossils have been found in southern England, Spain, Portugal and South Dakota, USA.

Camptosaurus skeleton

Othniel C. Marsh, the famous dinosaur hunter, named Camptosaurus in 1885 although it had first been discovered 1879. Camptosaurus seem to have been quite widespread as fossils have been found in Utah and Wyoming in the USA, and also in Oxfordshire in England, and in Portugal.

Camptosaurus was a heavy-bodied dinosaur, weighing up to 2,000 kg (2 tons), which could walk on all fours or rear up on its hind legs and balance to walk just on two feet. Standing, it could be up to 7 m (23 ft) tall. This was one of the first dinosaurs to have fleshy cheek pouches, like hamsters, for storing food in. It would have eaten **cycads**, ferns and needles from pine trees.

Dinosaur Data

PRONUNCIATION:	KAMP-TOE-SORE-USS
SUBORDER:	ORNITHOPODA
DIET:	BIPEDAL PLANT EATER

Permian period	Triassic period	Jurassic period	Cretaceous period
(290-248 million years ago)	(248-176 million years ago)	(176-130 million years ago)	(130-66 million years ago)

HYPSILOPHODON

High-ridged tooth

When it was first discovered in 1849 Hypsilophodon was thought to be a young Iguanodon (see page 156). However, in 1870 the **palaentologist** T.H. Huxley published a full description of Hypsilophodon and it was recognised as a different dinosaur.

Hypsilophodon was one of the smallest dinosaurs at around 2 m (6 ft) long and 70 kg (154 lb). It was **bipedal**, walking on two feet with only small forelimbs. Its heavy tail would have helped it to maintain its balance. It had 28 to 30 small, triangular, self-sharpening teeth to the front of its jaw for biting off leaves and ate low-growing plants and shrubs. Cheek pouches enabled it to store food for later, much like hamsters. Its small hands had five fingers each with four toes on each foot. Having a lightweight body would have enabled it to move quite fast for its size, helping it to escape from Baronyx (see page 60) and Megalosaurus (see page 80) which probably hunted it for food.

Hypsilohodon skeleton

At one time it was thought that Hypsilophodon may have lived in trees but this theory was later disproved.

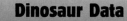

Dinosaur Data

PRONUNCIATION:	HIP-SILL-OWE-FOE-DON
SUBORDER:	ORNITHOPODA
DESCRIPTION:	LIGHTWEIGHT, FAST MOVER
DIET:	PLANT EATER

THESCELOSAURUS

Surprising reptile

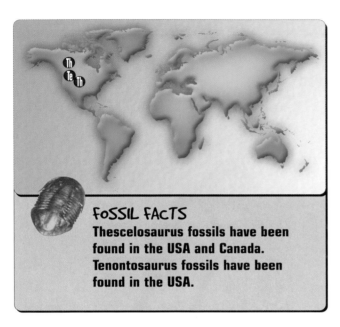

FOSSIL FACTS
Thescelosaurus fossils have been found in the USA and Canada. Tenontosaurus fossils have been found in the USA.

Thescelosaurus was first discovered in Wyoming in 1890 by John Bell Hatcher. The fossilised remains were simply left in crates to be discovered 22 years later in 1913 by Charles Gilmour who gave this creature a name.

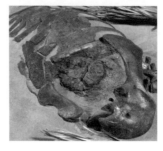

Fossilised dinosaur heart

Thescelosaurus was a sturdily-built **herbivore** measuring about 3.5–4 m (11–13 ft) and weighing up to 300 kg (660 lb). It had a small head, short front limbs, stout body, long hind legs with a powerful, long tapering tail which would have helped it to balance. It had a pointed beak and front teeth so, although it mainly ate plants, it would also have been able to eat some meat. Small **scutes** running along its back would have protected it from attack.

One specimen, found in 1993, was dated at 66 million years old. Unusually, these remains include a fossilised animal heart and some pieces of cartilage which are believed to be ribs in an almost complete specimen. Soft tissues are very rarely found, so some experts think that the fossilised heart is more likely to be a piece of rock. However, if it is the dinosaur's heart it can be seen to have four chambers, proving that this was a warm-blooded creature.

Thescelosaurus

Dinosaur Data

PRONUNCIATION:	THESS-KELL-OWE-SORE-USS
SUBORDER:	ORNITHOPODA
DESCRIPTION:	BIPEDAL HERBIVORE
DIET:	PLANTS

TENONTOSAURUS

Sinewy reptile

Tenontosaurus

Tenontosaurus was named by John Ostrom.

At 7.5 m (25 ft) high and weighing 900 kg (2,000 lb), Tenontosaurus was larger and heavier than other bird-footed dinosaurs. This made it almost three times their size. It also had a much longer tail. It is believed to be related to Iguanodon (see page 156) and Dryosaurus (see page 170).

Tenontosaurus probably walked on all fours and ate low-growing plants and shrubs.

Dinosaur Data

PRONUNCIATION:	TEN-ON-TOE-SORE-USS
SUBORDER:	ORNITHOPODA
DIET:	PLANT EATER

OTHNIELIA

Othniel's dinosaur

FOSSIL FACTS
Othinelia fossils have been discovered in Wyoming, Utah and Colorado, USA. Altirhinus fossils found in Mongolia.

Dinosaur Data

PRONUNCIATION:	OTH-NIGH-EEL-EE-AH
SUBORDER:	ORNITHOPODA
DESCRIPTION:	SMALL, AGILE **BIPEDAL** PLANT EATER

Othnielia would have walked upright on its long hind legs. Each back foot had four toes whilst its small hands had five fingers.

With its long thighs and feet it would probably have been quite a fast runner, enabling it to escape from predators fairly easily. Its tail, held off the ground, would have helped it to balance and make turns as it ran.

Othnielia

Peter Galton, the US-based British **palaeontologist** named this dinosaur in 1997 in honour of Professor Othniel Charles Marsh, the great 19th century dinosaur hunter, who himself named nearly 500 dinosaurs and other prehistoric animals.

This small bird-footed dinosaur is one of the smallest at only 1.5 m (5 ft) long and weighing only 20–25 kg (44–55 lb).

It had a small head and large eyes. It used its beak-like snout for tearing off leaves from low-growing vegetation and chewed with its chisel-like self-sharpening teeth. Like other bird-footed dinosaurs, Othnielia is believed to have had cheek pouches which it used for storing food for chewing later.

Othnielia fossil

Permian period	Triassic period	Jurassic period	
(290-248 million years ago)	(248-176 million years ago)	(176-130 million years ago)	

ALTIRHINUS

High nose

Originally thought to be a small Iguanodon (see page 156), Altirhinus was named in 1998 by David Norman, the British palaeontologist. With a body 8 m (26 ft) long and 4,000 kg (4 tons) in weight, Altirhinus was significantly smaller than Iguanodon, although similar in appearance.

Its skull was 75 cm (30 in.) long with a wide mouth for tearing at low-growing plants or grazing and a high arch at the top of its nose, which is how it got its name. Altirhinus would probably have walked and run on its hind legs but, when feeding on low-growing vegetation, it would probably have been on all fours even though its front legs were much shorter, about half the length, of its hind legs.

Fossilised remains of adults and a number of young Altirhinus have been discovered in the Dornogov province of Mongolia. The rocks in which they were found, the Khukhtek Formation, is known to have formed in the late Cretaceous period 100–125 million years ago. Other dinosaur fossils, Psittacosaurus (see page 152) and Shamosaurus, have also been found in the same rocks.

The distinctive tall arched nose of Altirhinus was made of bone and probably gave it a good sense of smell. It may also have helped to communicate with other Altirhnus through sound or sight. A further theory is that it would have been used for attracting a mate.

Altirhinus

Dinosaur Data

PRONUNCIATION:	ALL-TEE-RYNE-USS
SUBORDER:	ORNITHOPODA
DESCRIPTION:	BIPEDAL/QUADRUPEDAL PLANT EATER

169

DRYOSAURUS

Oak tree lizard

Dryosaurus was named in 1894 by the famous dinosaur hunter Othniel Charles Marsh. Having been found in a number of locations in the USA, Colorado, Wyoming and Utah, and Tanzania in Africa, it seems to have been fairly widespread.

Dinosaur Data

PRONUNCIATION:	DRY-OWE-SORE-USS
SUBORDER:	ORNITHOPODA
DESCRIPTION:	FOREST-DWELLING PLANT EATER

Dryosaurus had a long neck, long, slender legs, and a long, stiff tapering tail. Its arms were short with five fingers each and four toes on each foot. It was about 3 m (10 ft) long and 1.5 m (5 ft) tall. It would have weighed up to 80 kg (176 lb). Its strong legs would have made it a good runner and well-able to escape, most of the time, from the carnivorous dinosaurs which preyed on it.

Dryosaurus had a horny beak and long sharp cheek teeth which enabled it to chew its food thoroughly. It would have stored extra food in its cheek pouches for chewing later – like hamsters. It had quite large eyes and some experts believe that it had good eyesight.

It is thought to have been of average intelligence for a dinosaur when measured by brain to body ratio.

170

ORODROMEUS

Mountain runner

John Horner and David Weishampel named and described Orodromeus in 1988. Orodromeus was a small, lightweight dinosaur which was capable of moving quite fast. It lived in mountainous regions in Montana in the United States.

Dinosaur Data

PRONUNCIATION:	ORROW-DROM-EE-USS
SUBORDER:	ORITHOPODA
DESCRIPTION:	SMALL PLANT EATER

Orodromeus was less than 3 m (10 ft) in length and weighed only 10 kg (22 lb), so it was light but sturdy. Orodromeus had a beak-shaped mouth without front teeth but with cheek teeth which were self sharpening as they rubbed against each other when it was chewing its food. It would have eaten plants such as ferns and cycads. It had large eyes, a short neck and a sturdy body with small arms. Its hind legs were long and muscular and good for running.

Orodromeus lived at the same time as Tyrannosaurus Rex (see page 54) so it would have needed to have good eyesight and be able to run fast to avoid becoming its next meal.

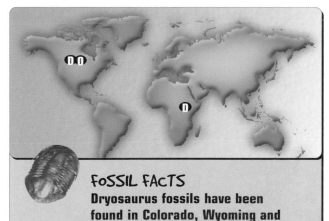

FOSSIL FACTS
Dryosaurus fossils have been found in Colorado, Wyoming and Utah, USA and Tanzania, Africa. Orodromeus fossils have been discovered in Montana, USA.

171

DISCOVERY OF FOSSILS

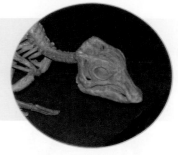

It is possible to find dinosaur remains anywhere that continental rocks were deposited at the end of the Triassic period and throughout the whole of the Jurassic and Cretaceous periods.

Common fossils

The most common fossils found are bones and teeth, because these are the hardest parts of the dinosaur. We have been able to find out about several different dinosaurs from their bones. Although the Tyrannosaurus Rex (see page 54) is not the biggest of the meat-eating dinosaurs (the Giganotosaurus, on page 56, is bigger), it is the most famous and is considered by many scientists to be the most important fossil of all time. The first Tyrannosurus Rex skeleton was discovered by **palaeontologist** Barnum Brown in Hell Creek, Montana, USA in 1902. The most complete Tyrannosaurus skeleton is nicknamed 'Sue'. She is now on display in Chicago's Field Museum.

Brachiosaurus (see page 94) fossils have been found in North America and Africa. The first Stegosaurus fossil was found in 1876 by M. P. Felch. Paleontologist Othniel C. Marsh named Stegosaurus in 1877. Many more Stegosaurus fossils have been found in western North America, western Europe, southern India, China, and southern Africa.

Many Triceratops fossils have been found, mostly in western Canada and the western United States. Paleontologist Othniel Marsh named Triceratops from a fossil found near

Denver, Colorado, USA, in 1889. At first this fossil was mistakenly identified as an extinct species of buffalo. The first Triceratops skull was found in 1888 by John Bell Hatcher. About 50 Triceratops skulls and some partial skeletons have been found.

Behaviour and lifestyle

We can learn much about a dinosaur's behaviour and lifestyle from their bones. For example, in 1927 a quarry in Utah, USA, was found to contain the skeletons of over 40 Allosaurus (see page 72) of all ages. Close examination of their skeletons show that they led a very rough life, and had lots of injuries and infections. One particularly large skeleton (nickname 'Big Al') revealed that the poor creature picked up dozens of injuries, particularly to its feet. Eventually the dinosaur would have ended up unable to walk or fend for itself, so it probably died of starvation or thirst.

Sue the Tyrannosaurus Rex skeleton from Chicago Field Museum

Brachoisarus fossil

Spike the Stegosaurus (Colorado) skeleton

Reconstruction

Fossils of Iguanodon (see page 156) were first found in southern England in 1822. It was one of the first dinosaurs to be identified by scientists, but early attempts at reconstructing its skeleton were a disaster and made it look like a rhino (the thumb spike was mistakenly placed on the nose). It was not until 1878, and the chance discovery of over 30 near-complete skeletons in Belgium, that Iguanodon was reconstructed with an upright stance.

Allosaurus skeleton

CORYTHOSAURUS

Crested duck-billed herbivore

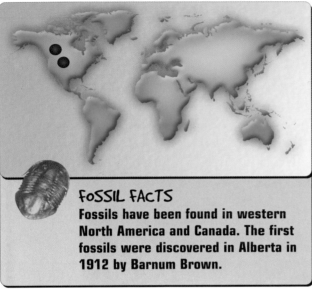

FOSSIL FACTS
Fossils have been found in western North America and Canada. The first fossils were discovered in Alberta in 1912 by Barnum Brown.

The purpose of Corythosaurus' helmet-shaped crests has been much debated by scientists. Some think that it served display purposes (adult males had larger head crests than juveniles or females) and recognising other Corythosaurus. Fossil remains of Corythosaursus have been found mixed together with those of other herbivores, suggesting that sometimes herds of different kinds of herbivore may have mingled together while migrating or grazing. If so, it would have been very useful to be able to recognise other members

Corythosaurus means 'helmet lizard'. This duck-billed dinosaur was named by Barnum Brown in 1914, for the hollow bony crest on top of its large head, shaped and flattened at the sides like a helmet.

Appearance

Corythosaurus grew to some 10 m (33 ft) long, standing 2 m (6 ft) high at the hip. It weighed around 4,000 kg (4 tons). Its arms were very much shorter than its back legs, and it is thought it could rise up on its hind legs and feet to look around for danger, and to run at a moderately fast pace. Its long pointed tail would help it balance. Fossilised footprints suggest that most of the time it went on all fours, foraging for low-growing plants. It would crop such plants with the toothless beak at the end of its long, narrow snout. Food would then be pushed back further, to be ground up by hundreds of sharp cheek teeth. These teeth were constantly replaced as they wore down and fell out.

of the Corythosaurus herd by looking for the distinctive crest on the head. Its enhanced sense of smell would also have helped it recognise and find its own kind.

Almost all scientists now agree that Corythosaurus also used the air chamber inside the crest to communicate by emitting sounds rather like a trumpet. The call of the Corythosaurus would have been booming and deep and carried great distances through the prehistoric forests.

MEGA FACTS

- In 1916, the Canadian ship *Mount Temple* was carrying two specimens of Corythosaurus from Canada to Britain when it was sunk by the German submarine *SMS Moewe*. Its prehistoric cargo now lies at the bottom of the North Atlantic.

- It is the duck-billed dinosaur about which we know most, since over 20 skulls have been found.

- Scientists once thought this dinosaur lived mostly in the water, as it appeared to have webbed feet and hands. Later study showed that the 'webs' were simply deflated padding.

- Corythosaurus lived between the western mountains of North America and an inland sea. It may have migrated from the shoreline to higher ground to reproduce.

Dinosaur Data

PRONUNCIATION:	COR-**IH**-THOH-**SAWR**-US
SUBORDER:	ORNITHOPODA
FAMILY:	HADROSAURIDAE
DESCRIPTION:	CRESTED HERBIVORE
FEATURES:	HELMET-SHAPED CREST
DIET:	PINE NEEDLES, CONIFERS, GINKGOS, TWIGS, LEAVES, FRUITS

175

MAIASAURA

Migratory duck-billed dinosaur

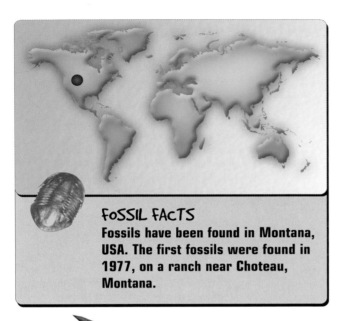

FOSSIL FACTS
Fossils have been found in Montana, USA. The first fossils were found in 1977, on a ranch near Choteau, Montana.

It grew to around 9.2 m (30 ft) long and weighed 3,000–4,000 kg (3–4 tons) when fully grown. It went on all four legs most of the time, but may have been able to raise up onto its hind legs to reach vegetation or to run away from predators. Its arms were much shorter than the strong back legs.

Family life

Large numbers of fossils from this dinosaur have been found together (one site contained 10,000!) including eggs, nests and babies. Scientists therefore believe Maiasaura was a herding animal. The discovery of this dinosaur revolutionised the way we think about how dinosaurs raised their young, challenging the traditional view of them as uncaring reptiles that largely left their eggs and young to fend for themselves.

The most famous find was made on a site that has become known as 'Egg Mountain'. This site had preserved a group of Maiasaura nests, and one of these contained bones from

Maiasaura means 'good mother lizard'. It was named by **palaeontologist** Jack Horner, after he discovered a series of nests with the remains of both eggs and hatchlings in them. This was the first proof that some giant dinosaurs raised and fed their young.

Appearance

Maiasaura was a **hadrosaur** that inhabited the coastal lowlands of Montana some 75 million years ago. Unlike some hadrosaurs, it had only a tiny crest on its head – it also had small bony spikes above each eye. Its face was long and broad, ending in a short, wide bill. Its flat skull measured up to 82 cm (33 in.) long and 35 cm (14 in.) high. Its beak was toothless, but Maiasaura had many self-sharpening teeth further back in it cheeks to grind up vegetation.

Permian period	Triassic period	Jurassic period	Cretaceous period
(290-248 million years ago)	**(248-176 million years ago)**	**(176-130 million years ago)**	**(130-66 million years ago)**

Maiasaura skeleton

babies some weeks old. That these babies were still in the nest so long after hatching showed that the parent dinosaurs must have been looking after them. Babies were about 35 cm (14 in.) long when they hatched and grew to 3 m (10 ft) by the end of their first year, an impressively fast rate of growth.

Large amounts of plant remains have been found around fossilised eggs, and in fact vegetation may have been placed over the eggs to help incubate them – the rotting vegetation would generate heat.

MEGA FACTS

- In 1985, a bone fragment from Maiasaura was flown into space during an eight-day NASA experiment for Skylab 2.

- Maiasaura is the official state fossil of Montana.

Dinosaur Data

PRONUNCIATION:	**MY**-AH-**SAWR**-AH
SUBORDER:	ORNITHOPODA
FAMILY:	HADROSAURIDAE
DESCRIPTION:	MEDIUM-SIZED DUCK-BILLED DINOSAUR
FEATURES:	TINY SKULL CREST, LARGE SKULL, BROAD BILL
DIET:	LOW-GROWING VEGETATION AND SOME HIGHER LEAVES

EDMONTOSAURUS

Toothy duck-billed tree browser

D U C K B I L L S

Edmontosaurus means 'lizard from Edmonton'. It was named in 1917.

Appearance

Edmontosarous was 13 m (43 ft) long and weighed around 3,500 kg 3.5 tons. It had the flat and sloping head common to many duck-billed dinosaurs, and its mouth was a wide spoon-like beak.

The beak was toothless, but packed tightly back in the cheeks were six rows containing hundreds of teeth – Edmontosaurus would have been able to grind up very tough food by moving it across these teeth and back from muscular cheek pouches. As soon as a tooth wore out, it was replaced.

This tree-browsing **herbivore** would have gone on all four legs to graze, but was probably able to stand up on its powerful hind legs and move on just those two legs. Its front legs were shorter and less powerful.

FOSSIL FACTS
Fossils have been found in the USA and Canada. The first fossils were discovered in 1912.

Dinosaur Data

PRONUNCIATION:	ED-MON-TOE-SAWR-US
SUBORDER:	ORNITHOPODA
FAMILY:	HADROSAURIDAE
DESCRIPTION:	TREE-BROWSING DUCK-BILLED DINOSAUR
FEATURES:	HUNDREDS OF TEETH, LOOSE SKIN BALLOON
DIET:	CONIFER NEEDLES, SEEDS, TWIGS

Edmontosaurus

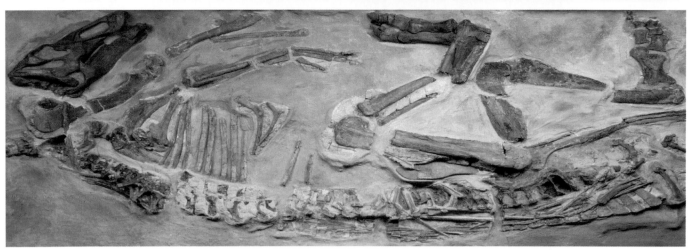

Edmontosaurus skeleton

Defence

Edmontosaurus was slow-moving, and possessed few defences – it may have had good eyesight, hearing and smell to help it keep out of the way of predators who shared the same time and territory, such as Tyrannosaurus Rex (see page 54). We also know, from some remarkable mummified fossil remains found in 1908, that Edmontosaurus had tough, scaly skin, with a row of bumps (called tubercles) running along its neck, back and tail.

With few ways to defend themselves, these herbivores were likely to have sought safety by banding together in herds. In Alberta (Canada) a mass 'graveyard' of Edmontosaurus fossils supports the idea that they lived in herds. They may have migrated with the seasons, from the North Slope of Alaska (where plants to eat would have been scarce in the dark months of winter) to the richer, swampy area of Alberta.

MEGA FACTS

- An Edmontosaurus fossil now displayed in the Denver Museum of Nature and Science shows evidence of a Tryannosaurus Rex bite to the tail. Astonishingly, the bone shows signs of healing – the Edmontosaurus apparently lived through the attack. This evidence of healing proved that Tyrannosaurus Rex's prey was alive when bitten, which means Tryannosaurus Rex was not a pure scavenger as was suggested in the 1970s.

- As Edmontosaurus herds migrated, Tryannosaurus Rex probably followed its food source, snatching weaker or older members of the herd as "ready meals."

- When first found, many scientists thought Edmontosaurus must have spent a lot of its time in the water, as is hands seemed to be webbed. None of the other evidence we have argues for an aquatic lifestyle, however, and it seems that the "webs" were simply collapsed padding that had once cushioned the feet and hands.

PARASAUROLOPHUS

Toothy duck-billed tree-browser

FOSSIL FACTS
Fossils have been found in Canada and the USA. The first fossil was found in Alberta in 1922.

Parasaurolophus means 'near crested lizard'. It was named by Dr William A. Parks, in 1922. It lived in the jungles of North America 75–65 million years ago.

Appearance

Parasaurolophus had the most remarkable skull crest of any of its kind. The crest extending from the back of its skull could be up to 1.8 m (10 ft) long and was a hollow tube filled with passages that connected its nostrils right back to the tip of the crest.

Parasaurolophus was one of the largest **herbivores** of the Cretaceous period. It grew up to 10 m (33 ft) long and 4.9 m (16 ft) high, and weighed around 3,500 kg (3.5 tons). Its front legs were shorter than its back legs – it probably went on all fours when foraging for low-growing plants, but could rise up onto its back legs, using its long tail to help balance, to look around, reach higher leaves, or run away from predators. It had no real

Dinosaur Data

PRONUNCIATION:	PAR-AH-**SAWR**-OH-**??**-FUSS
SUBORDER:	ORNITHOPODA
FAMILY:	HADROSAURIDAE
DESCRIPTION:	BIZARRELY-CRESTED DUCKBILLED HERBIVORE
FEATURES:	MASSIVE SKULL CREST
DIET:	LEAVES, TWIGS, PINE-NEEDLES

means to defend itself besides running away, and probably sought safety in numbers by living in herds.

Its long neck would allow it to reach food either on the ground or up in the trees.

It had a duck-like beak at the front of its snout that would allow it to slice off leaves and other vegetation – all its teeth were further back, in its cheeks, where food would be pushed to be ground up into mush. Its snout was narrow, and shorter than those of most other duckbilled dinosaurs.

Parasaurolophus' 'voice'

Parasaurolophus' amazing crest contained a maze of air chambers that connected back to the breathing passages.

Most scientists believe this allowed the crest to be used as a 'resonating chamber', which let the dinosaur make loud, low-frequency sounds by blowing air through it. In 1995 a study in New Mexico was begun using powerful computers and CT scans of a fossil skull to

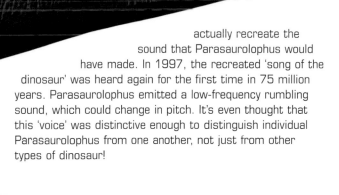

actually recreate the sound that Parasaurolophus would have made. In 1997, the recreated 'song of the dinosaur' was heard again for the first time in 75 million years. Parasaurolophus emitted a low-frequency rumbling sound, which could change in pitch. It's even thought that this 'voice' was distinctive enough to distinguish individual Parasaurolophus from one another, not just from other types of dinosaur!

MEGA FACTS

- Its brain was about the size of a human fist.

- Fossils of the large bones in its ears suggest it would have been able to hear sounds below the range of human hearing.

- Fossil remains have shown us that Parasaurolophus' hide was tough and pebbly.

Parasaurolophus skeleton

GRYPOSAURUS

Griffin lizard

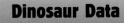

FOSSIL FACTS

Fossils have been found in Canada and the USA and, possibly, South America.

Gryposaurus was named by the Canadian **paleontologist** Lawrence Lambe in 1914.

When first discovered, Gryposaurus was believed to have been Kritosaurus, a very similar-looking dinosaur, also found in Canada and Argentina, which was named in 1910. Its name, which it was given because of its elegant appearance, means "reptile". There are also at least two other dinosaurs, Trachodon, discovered in 1856, and Naashoibitosaurus, discovered in 1993, which have been found in the same locations and are all very similar to each other.

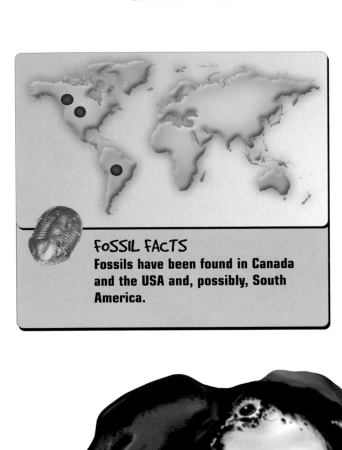

Dinosaur Data

PRONUNCIATION:	GRIP-OWE-SORE-USS
SUBORDER:	ORNITHOPODA
FAMILY:	HADROSAUR
DESCRIPTION:	DUCK-BILLED PLANT EATER

Permian period	Triassic period	Jurassic period	Cretaceous period
(290-248 million years ago)	(248-176 million years ago)	(176-130 million years ago)	(130-66 million years ago)

At around 9 m (30 ft) tall and weighing up to 3,000 kg (3 tons), Gryposaurus is regarded as a medium-sized hadrosaur. Fossilised skulls and bones show that Gryposaurus would have had a very distinctively shaped nose with very curved upward-facing nostrils and a very prominent and angular nose. The head itself was long and narrow with a characteristic duck bill jaw.

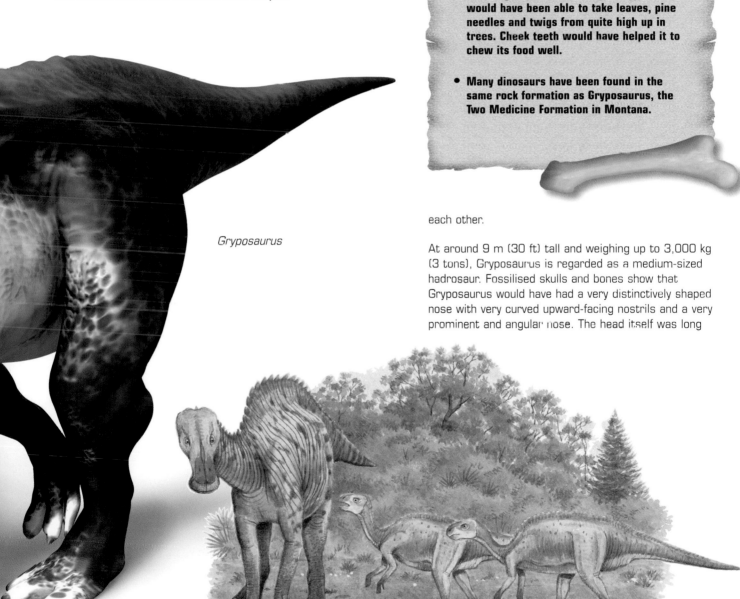

Gryposaurus

MEGA FACTS

- Standing tall on its hind legs, Gryposaurus would have been able to take leaves, pine needles and twigs from quite high up in trees. Cheek teeth would have helped it to chew its food well.

- Many dinosaurs have been found in the same rock formation as Gryposaurus, the Two Medicine Formation in Montana.

each other.

At around 9 m (30 ft) tall and weighing up to 3,000 kg (3 tons), Gryposaurus is regarded as a medium-sized hadrosaur. Fossilised skulls and bones show that Gryposaurus would have had a very distinctively shaped nose with very curved upward-facing nostrils and a very prominent and angular nose. The head itself was long

183

HYPACROSAURUS

Very high lizard

The front of its mouth, which was flat, lacked teeth although it had 40 rows of teeth at the back of its jaw which were strong enough to chew even the toughest plants and shrubs around.

Hypacrosaurus had large eyes and a good sense of smell which would have helped it to sense and keep clear of predators such as Tyrannosaurus Rex (see page 54) and Albertosaurus.

Very young, recently-hatched Hypacrosaurus eggs and nests, the biggest collection of baby skeletons of any hadrosaur ever found, were discovered at Glacier Creek in Montana.

FOSSIL FACTS
Hypacrosaurus fossils have been found in Montana, USA and Alberta, Canada.

Hypacrosaurus was named by American fossil hunter Barnum Brown in 1913.

It looked very like Corythosaurus (see page 174) although its crest was lower, narrower and a less-rounded shape. It would have been about 9 m (30 ft) long and 2,000–3,000 kg (2–3 tons) in weight.

Hypacrosaurus had large powerful back legs equipped with three hooves each, while its front legs were smaller but still able to bear its weight when walking or running. Its hands had four fingers each.

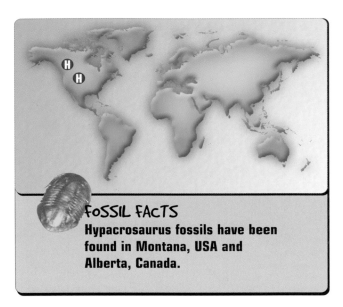

Dinosaur Data

PRONUNCIATION:	HIGH-PAH-KROE-SORE-USSS
SUBORDER:	ORNITHOPODA
FAMILY:	HADROSAUR
DESCRIPTION:	LARGE EYED PLANT EATER

Hypacrosaurus ate a wide range of vegetation from ground level (e.g. pine needles, flowering plants) up to a height of 4m (13 ft). Using a combination of its large mouth and the teeth at the back of its jaws, it could grind up even the toughest of plants. These teeth were constantly replaced – the Hypacrosaurus could have hundreds of teeth at any one time, with only a few being used.

Like the adult Hypacrosaurus, its young were large, measuring 1.7m (5.5 ft) at hatching, eventually reaching their full size of 9m (30 ft) long by the age of 12 years. This represents a rapid growth rate compared to the Tyrannosaurus, for example, which didn't reach its full size until roughly 25 years of age.

The purpose of the Hypacrosaurus's distinctive crest has been the subject of debate, with some experts suggesting that its main function was social, while others have put forward the idea that it acted as a resonating chamber to amplify the dinosaur's roar. Males had longer crests than females or juveniles.

MEGA FACTS

- This dinosaur's full species name is Hypacrosaurus Altispinus, meaning "nearly the highest lizard", because when it was discovered, it was thought to be one of the largest dinosaurs. Subsequently many larger dinosaurs have been discovered. The 'altispinus' refers to the height of the 'fin' running along its spine. A second species was described in the 1990s.

- Hypacrosaurus could stand on two or four feet; when running it stood on its hind legs, but probably remained on all four when foraging for food.

- Hypacrosaurus may have lived in herds.

- Hadrosaurs were the most common dinosaurs in the Northern Hemisphere during the late Cretaceous Period.

FORMATION OF FOSSILS

A fossil means the traces of any past life preserved in the rocks. Fossilisation takes millions of years. When a dinosaur died, normally the bones started to fall apart. If, however, the body was quickly covered with a layer of earth, this process did not occur.

Once the sediment had covered the dinosaur, its soft parts disappeared over time and only the hard bones and teeth were left behind.

The sediment gradually built up on top of the bones, forming part of rocks such as limestone, mudstone, sandstone, clay or shale. Minerals from water around the rocks seeped into the bone structure, which gradually changed into rock.

Millions of years later the fossil appeared as the covering rock was worn away by wind and water.

There are only a few fossils of dinosaurs because they were land animals, and it is normally sea creatures that were fossilised as the silt at the bottom of the sea or a lake covered the remains.

How fossils are made

There are a number of ways in which dinosaur remains can become fossils. When sediment covers bones and minerals seep into the bones, it gradually turns into rock. These fossils, part original bone and part rock, are called 'petrified'.

Ankylosaurus

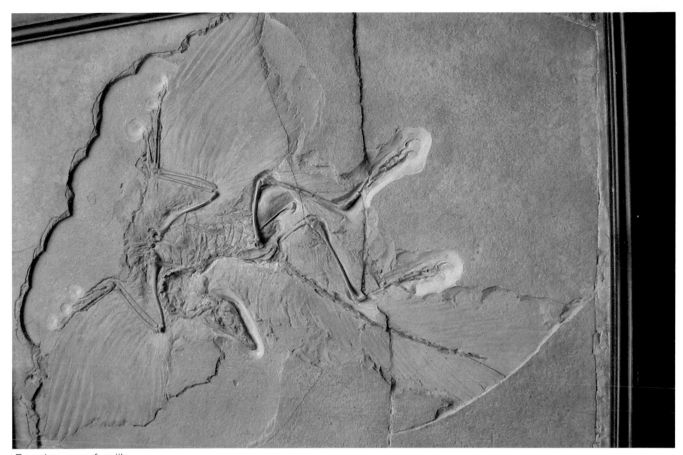

Ramphoryncus fossiils

Sometimes acidic water dissolved the bone and left a hollow space (mould) where the bone used to be. These are 'natural mould' fossils and, by pouring material such as plaster of Paris or rubber latex into them, the exact shape of the bone can be recreated.

In other cases, these natural moulds are filled later with sediments or different minerals such as silica, calcite or iron pyrites which gradually built up a perfect copy (replica). These are 'natural cast' fossils.

Sometimes a dead animal is buried between layers of rock, which form an impression or cast that can be split apart along the layer containing the bones, producing a part and counterpart. In a few cases, the casts include impressions of feathers or skin that decayed long ago.

The rarest fossil of all formed when the dinosaur's body had been covered in a dry environment and some of the soft parts had become preserved (mummified) and then fossilised. In these cases, the skin texture, and even the folds in it, can be clearly seen. The colour is not preserved though as it takes on the colour of the surrounding rocks.

Construction of a replica skeleton of Titanosaurus

Other fossils

Apart from dinosaur remains, other fossils of the dinosaurs exist, such as fossilised footprints or tracks, nests and eggs, scratches in the ground, toothmarks on bones, dung, stomach stones and much more. These can tell us about how the dinosaurs lived and behaved, not just what they looked like. For example, footprints and tracks tell us whether dinosaurs lived alone or in groups, and how fast they moved.

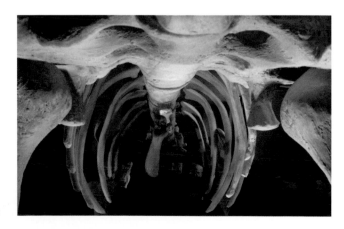

DIMORPHODON

Primitive fish-eating winged reptile

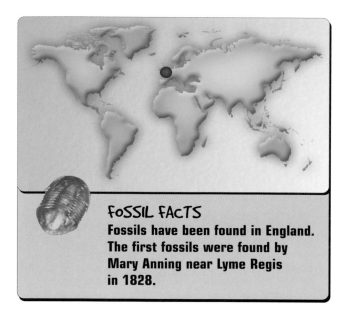

FOSSIL FACTS
Fossils have been found in England. The first fossils were found by Mary Anning near Lyme Regis in 1828.

The name Dimorphodon means 'two-form teeth'. It was named by **palaeontologist** Sir Richard Owen in 1859. It has two distinct kinds of teeth – those at the front are longer than those at the back.

Appearance

Dimorphodon was actually a winged reptile called a **pterosaur** that lived at the same time as the dinosaurs. It is one of the earliest pterosaurs that have been discovered, living 206–180 million years ago, and quite a small one at 1 m (3 ft) long. Its wings were formed by a leathery membrane which stretched between its body, the top of its legs and its fourth finger. Its hollow bones made it light in the air.

It had a massive head, with wide and deep jaws. The head was extremely large compared to the rest of the body, and it is thought the large beak may have been coloured, making it useful for display to other Dimorphodons. Like all pterosaurs, it had huge eyes and so probably excellent eyesight.

At the other end of its body was a long, pointed tail, which ended in a curious diamond-shaped flap of skin. This tail may have helped stabilise the creature while in the air, or helped to balance it while walking on the ground.

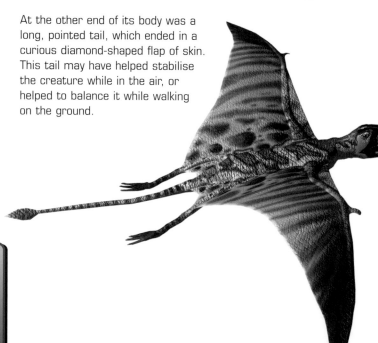

Dinosaur Data

PRONUNCIATION:	DIE-**MORF**-OH-DON
SUBORDER:	RHAMPHORYNCHOIDEA
FAMILY:	DIMORPHODONTIDAE
DESCRIPTION:	PRIMITIVE WINGED REPTILE
FEATURES:	TWO DIFFERENT KINDS OF TEETH IN ITS BEAK
DIET:	FISH, INSECTS AND POSSIBLY SMALL ANIMALS

MEGA FACTS

- It had a wingspan of 6 ft (1.7m).

- The specimen found by Mary Anning is believed to have been the first complete pterosaur skeleton ever discovered.

- It may have used its increased leg span to hold onto cliffs while waiting for fish to surface – then swooped down to catch its next meal.

Dimorphodon skull

How it moved

There is disagreement about how Dimorphodon moved when it was not flying. Fossil tracks seem to suggest that it went on all fours, but some scientists think it was capable of standing fully or semi-upright on its hind legs and even running quite fast. Unlike most other pterosaurs, Dimorphodon had legs which rather stuck out to the sides, which would have given it a somewhat clumsy, waddling gait. This leads some **palaeontologists** to suggest it may have spent most of its time off the ground, hanging from tree branches or cliffs, using its grasping hands and toe claws to hold on.

It has often been thought that Dimorphodon would have been able to run very fast, rising up onto its toes to do so. Recently-discovered fossil evidence, though, suggests that it was actually incapable of bending its foot – it would have been flat-footed and needed to place either all or none of its foot on the ground.

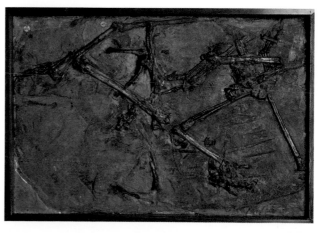

Dimorphodon fossilised skeleton

189

CAUDIPTERYX

Flightless feathered dinosaur

FOSSIL FACTS
Fossils were found in the Liaoning Province of China in 1997 and identified by Philip Currie.

Caudipteryx means 'tail feather' or 'winged tail' and refers to this dinosaur's short, feathered tail plume.

Appearance

Caudipteryx was a small **bipedal** dinosaur, with long legs, a pair of very short arms and a short tail. It was about 1 m (3 ft) tall and weighed about the same as a large turkey. Its short snout contained long sharp teeth. Its long legs and relatively light weight would have made it a very fast runner.

Its body was covered in short, downy feathers and had longer, quill-like feathers on its arms and tail. The tail feathers were up to 20 cm (8 in.) long and arranged in a fan or plume. It is thought that Caudipteryx could have used this tail plume for display. Although Caudipteryx's arms had long, quill-like feathers and looked much more like small wings than arms, it could not fly.

Caudipteryx's feathers were still very useful to it as they would have provided good insulation. They may have also have been useful for aggressive displays or to attract a mate, as well as allowing it to warm its eggs.

Diet

Caudipteryx lived in wetlands, so it probably waded in the water to catch small fish in its sharp-toothed mouth. However, fossils have been found with tiny stones in their stomach. These gastroliths are used to help digest vegetable matter, suggesting its diet consisted at least partially of plants. It is possible that it had a diet consisting of plants, small fish and other small animals.

Dinosaur Data

PRONUNCIATION:	CAW-**DIP**-TER-IKS
SUBORDER:	THEROPODA
FAMILY:	CAUDIPTERIDAE
DESCRIPTION:	LONG-LEGGED FEATHERED DINOSAUR
FEATURES:	DISTINCTIVE TAIL PLUME, FEATHERS AND WING-LIKE ARMS
DIET:	SMALL FISH

MEGA FACTS

- Caudipteryx's teeth faced outward, giving it a distinctly buck-toothed appearance.

- Caudipteryx is one of many excellent fossil samples to have been discovered in the Liaoning province of China. These finds are especially exciting because of their excellent state of preservation — some even have impressions of skin and feathers, even indicating patterns like banding that help us to understand what dinosaurs really looked like.

Evolution of Birds

Most scientists now accept that birds evolved from dinosaurs. However, some believe that all birds descended from a creature called Archaeopteryx (see page 192). Others believe that modern birds evolved from the maniraptors, a group whose early members included Caudipteryx and whose later members included Velociraptor (see page 66) and Deinonychus (see page 58). These later members had evolved the swivelling wrist bone joint that is necessary for flight.

Caudipteryx's feathers and wing-like arms suggest that it might be the missing link in the evolution of birds from dinosaurs!

ARCHAEOPTERYX

Winged and feathered bipedal carnivore

**F
L
Y
I
N
G

D
I
N
O
S
A
U
R
S**

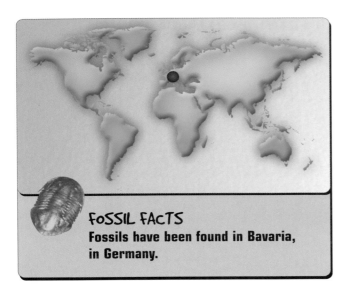

FOSSIL FACTS
Fossils have been found in Bavaria, in Germany.

Bird-like features	Dinosaur-like features
Feathered wings with reduced finger	Claws on wings, could be used to grasp
Wishbone	Teeth
Bird-like brain	Long bony tail
Hollow bones	Jaws (not a beak!)
Feathers on body and tail	

This table gives details of the features that Archaeopteryx shared with birds and dinosaurs.

Archaeopteryx means 'ancient feather'. It was named by Hermann von Meyer in 1861. Archaeopteryx is often said to be a link between dinosaurs and birds.

In 2004, an experiment was carried out at the National History Museum in London to try to answer this question. Scanning equipment was used to scan the brain case of an Archaeopteryx skull. The brain shape was much more like that of a modern bird than the brain of a dinosaur.

Appearance

Archaeopteryx was magpie-sized, weighing around 325 g (12 oz). It had short, broad wings and a long tail and neck. Its jaws were lined with sharp cone-shaped teeth. It had long legs, with long thighs and short calves. Its wings, body and tail were feathered. Its large eyes would have given it excellent vision. It had feathers and wings like a bird, but teeth, skeleton and claws like a dinosaur.

In 2005, a particularly well-preserved fossil specimen was studied. The second toe could be stretched much more t han the rest, rather like the special 'retractable' claws of Velociraptor (see page 66). The hind toe was not 'reversed' like a thumb on a grasping hand, and so Archaeopteryx could not have used it to cling onto branches.

Could Archaeopteryx fly?

Scientists have argued over whether or not this animal could fly ever since the first Archaeopteryx fossil was found. If it could fly, did it just flap its wings weakly, or fly strongly?

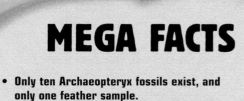

Archaeopteryx fossil

MEGA FACTS

- Only ten Archaeopteryx fossils exist, and only one feather sample.

- Archaeopteryx's brain was only the size of a conker. But the size of its brain compared to its body was three times as big as that of similar sized reptiles.

- It had a wingspan of 50 cm (18 in.).

- There were flying dinosaurs before and after Archaeopteryx, but they had skin, not feathers, on their wings.

The areas controlling vision and movements were enlarged, just like a bird's, and the inner ear (which controls balance) was also like a bird's. It was a brain designed for flight and balance!

Dr Angela Milner, who carried out the study, believes this is strong evidence that Archaeopteryx could and did fly. Most scientists now agree that archaeopteryx *could* fly, but was a weak flyer.

Dinosaur Data

PRONUNCIATION:	ARK-EE**OP**-TER-IKS
SUBORDER:	THERAPODA
FAMILY:	ARCHAEOPTERIDAE
DESCRIPTION:	FEATHERED BIPEDAL CARNIVORE
FEATURES:	FEATHERED WINGS
DIET:	INSECTS, SMALL CREATURES

PTERANODON INGENS

Winged and toothless flying reptile

F
L
Y
I
N
G

D
I
N
O
S
A
U
R
S

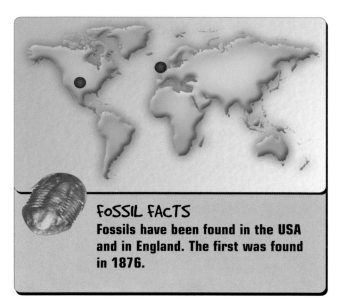

FOSSIL FACTS
Fossils have been found in the USA and in England. The first was found in 1876.

Dinosaur Data

PRONUNCIATION:	TER-AN-O-DON
SUBORDER:	PTERODACTYLOIDEA
FAMILY:	PTERADONTIDAE
DESCRIPTION:	CARNIVORE
FEATURES:	HUGE WINGSPAN
DIET:	FISH, MOLLUSCS, CRABS, INSECTS

It probably looked more like a huge bat than a bird with large soft hair covered membranes for wings. The membrane itself was very thin but extremely strong and stretched out between the body and the tops of its legs. These flying reptiles did not have any feathers.

Pteranodon lived at the same time as Tyrannosaurus Rex. It was not a true dinosaur but was related to them.

Pteranodon had a wing span of up to 9–10 m (30–33 ft) and weighed around 20–25 kg (44–55 lb).

It would have been able to walk on the ground but, once in the air, Pteranodon would have looked like a huge glider. Pteranodon could fly long distances using its large light-weight wings; it would have taken advantage of rising thermals to soar over the swampy forest below.

MEGA FACTS

- It used the large bony crest on its head to steer when flying.

- Their brightly-coloured crests were larger in the male and were used for attracting females and indicating readiness to mate.

- Their lower jaw was over 1m (3 ft) in length.

- They would have been agile, elegant and quite fast when flying, reaching speeds up to 48 km/h (30 mph).

Diet

It had no teeth but was **carnivorous**. Fossil skeletons found near the edge of the sea show that fish was probably an important part of its diet. Its scoop-like beak would have helped it to swoop down to catch fish straight from near the surface of the water. Its excellent eyesight would have helped it to see fish in the water as it flew above the surface.

HESPERORNIS

Flightless toothed marine dinosaur

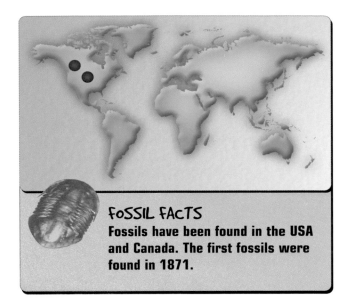

Appearance

Hesperornis looked a lot like a bird with teeth. It grew to about 1.5 m (5 ft) long and it had small and useless wings (which scientists call *vestigal* wings). It had sprawling back legs, set very far back on the body. These long legs ended in webbed feet. It had a big head on the end of a long neck. Its long beak was set with simple, sharp teeth along its bottom jaw, and at the back of its upper jaw.

A different kind of hesperornithiform, called Parahesperornis, has been found showing the imprinted remains of thick, hairy feathers. It is likely that Hesperornis, too, had such feathers. They would not have helped it fly, but would have done a good job of keeping it warm.

In the water, Hesperornis was a powerful swimmer and diver. Unlike modern flightless birds like penguins, it did not use its wings as well as its feet to push itself through the water. Its wings were tiny and of no use, but its back

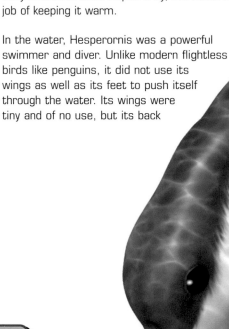

Hesperornis means 'western bird'. It was named in 1871 by the **palaeontologist** Othniel C. Marsh. The discovery of Hesperornis was very important, because it filled a big gap in the fossil history of birds.

Hesperornis is part of a group of dinosaurs called the hesperornithiforms. These were the only true marine dinosaurs of the whole Mesozoic era. Dinosaurs that lived in the sea seem to have lived only in the northern hemisphere and were flightless diving birds. They would have dived to catch fish.

Dinosaur Data

PRONUNCIATION:	**HES**-PER-**OR**-NIS
SUBORDER:	ODONTORNITHES
FAMILY:	HESPERORNITHIDAE
DESCRIPTION:	FLIGHTLESS TOOTHED DIVING BIRD
FEATURES:	VESTIGAL WINGS, TOOTHED BEAK
DIET:	FISH, SQUID, AMMONITES

Permian period	Triassic period	Jurassic period	Cretaceous period
(290-248 million years ago)	(248-176 million years ago)	(176-130 million years ago)	(130-66 million years ago)

legs were powerful. The wings may have been useful for steering when diving underwater. It had dense (heavy) bones that made it less buoyant and helped it to dive. Its sleek, feathered body was well designed for moving smoothly through the water.

On land, Hesperornis was awkward and clumsy. Thanks to the position of its hip bones and back legs, it may not even have been able to stand up and waddle about on dry land. It would have moved on land by sliding about on its belly, pushing with those strong back legs.

It probably only went up on land to nest and lay eggs. For safety, it probably nested in groups, and chose inaccessible, rocky spots.

MEGA FACTS

- Hesperornis remains have been found in the fossilised stomachs of mosasaur (see page 42) skeletons.

- Hesperornis was the largest of the flightless diving birds of the late Cretaceous period.

- Unable to fly or walk, Hesperornis was in danger from predators both in the water and on land.

RHAMPHORYNCUS

Flying reptile

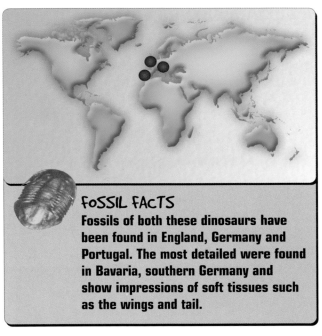

FOSSIL FACTS

Fossils of both these dinosaurs have been found in England, Germany and Portugal. The most detailed were found in Bavaria, southern Germany and show impressions of soft tissues such as the wings and tail.

Rhamphorhynchus was a pterosaur, which lived during the late Jurassic period. It had a wingspan up to 1.75 m (6 ft). The wings were made of thin skin stretched between an elongated finger from its hand, down to its ankle.

Rhamphorhynchus had a long, thin and pointed tail. At the end of its tail it had a flap of skin, which was diamond shaped. This helped with its balance in flight.

Rhamphorhynchus also had long and thin jaws with incredibly sharp teeth, probably for catching fish. It is believed that one of the ways Rhamphorhynchus hunted was by dragging its beak in the water in the hope of coming into contact with fish, then it would snap its needle-sharp teeth shut and toss the food into its throat pouch. It probably wouldn't have hunted on land as it only had tiny legs, which would have made it a poor runner.

Dinosaur Data

PRONUNCIATION:	**RAM**-FOR-**INK**-US
SUBORDER:	RHAMPHORHYNCHOIDEA
FAMILY:	RHAMPHORHYNCHIDAE
DESCRIPTION:	FLYING REPTILE
FEATURES:	BIRD-LIKE MEAT EATER
DIET:	FISH, MOLLUSKS, INSECTS

PTEROSAUR

Flying reptile

Dinosaur Data

PRONUNCIATION:	TER-OH-**SAW**
SUBORDER:	PTERODACTYLOIDEA
FAMILY:	PTEROSAUR
DESCRIPTION:	FLYING REPTILES
FEATURES:	BIRD-LIKE MEAT EATERS
DIET:	FISH, MOLLUSKS, INSECTS

Pterosaurs were flying reptiles and they lived from the late Triassic period to the end of the Cretaceous period, 228 to 65 million years ago. Pterosaurs were the first vertebrates that were able to fly. When Pterosaurs were first discovered, it was thought that they lived in water. However, in the 19th century Georges Cuvier proposed that pterosaurs flew.

Pterosaur wings were covered with a tough and leathery membrane that stretched between its body, the top of its legs and its fourth finger.

MEGA FACTS

- Pterosaur bones were hollow, just like those of birds.

- Pterosaurs had large brains and good eyesight.

- Some pterosaurs were covered in a type of hair, or fibres.

- Competition with early bird species may have resulted in the extinction of many of the Pterosaurs.

There were many different types of pterosaurs and their wing designs differed. This meant that some of the species flapped their wings and could fly with great power. Others simply glided through the air, relying on updrafts of warm air to help them fly.

Quite a few species of pterosaurs had webbed feet, which could have been used for swimming, but some believe that they were used to help gliding pterosaurs.

When the great extinction wiped out all the dinosaurs at the end of the Cretaceous period, the pterosaurs also disappeared.

199

QUETZALCOATLUS

Feathered serpent god

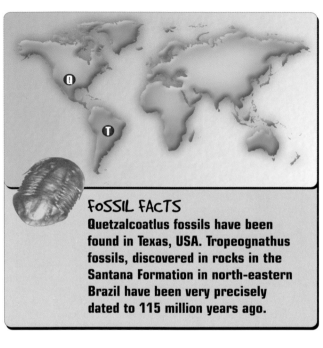

FOSSIL FACTS

Quetzalcoatlus fossils have been found in Texas, USA. Tropeognathus fossils, discovered in rocks in the Santana Formation in north-eastern Brazil have been very precisely dated to 115 million years ago.

Living at the same time as Tyrannosaurus Rex (see page 54) and Triceratops (see page 136) it would have been an impressive sight as it swooped down low over the swampy wetlands of the southern US scavenging for food. Its enormous size made it four times larger than today's scavenging birds, the condors and vultures.

Its outstretched neck was 3 m (10 ft) long with a slim, pointed toothless beak 2 m (6 ft) long. On the top of its head was a short, bony crest. At the front of its wings were small three fingered hands equipped with sharp claws. Swept behind it as it flew were its vast feet – each larger than an adult human's leg.

Quetzalcoatlus was named in 1975 after the Aztec feathered serpent god, although Quetzalcoaltus itself probably didn't have any feathers, just fine fur like a bat.

As with other pterasaurs, and birds today, its hollow bones would have helped it to fly and remain airborne despite its vast size. Using rising thermals to soar through the air, Quetzalcoatlus would have fed on fish or scavenged on rotting carcasses it found around the water's edge.

With a wingspan of 12 m (39 ft), maybe more, it was one of the largest flying animals ever to have lived. It would have weighed around 70 kg (154 lb) – the same sort of weight as an adult human.

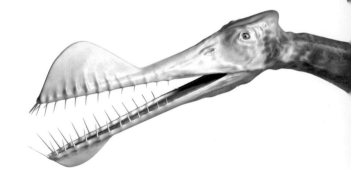

TROPEOGNATHUS

Keel jaw

Dinosaur Data

PRONUNCIATION:	KETT-ZAL-COE-AT-LUSS
SUBORDER:	PTERASAURIA
DESCRIPTION:	LARGE SCAVENGING BIRD
DIET:	FISH, SHELLFISH AND MEAT

With a wingspan of 6 m (20 ft), Tropeognathus was a very large flying reptile.

At 12–14 kg (26–31 lb) it was much lighter than Queztalcoatlus and better suited to preying on fish and squid at the surface of lakes and swamps. It could feed like a flamingo trailing its beak in the water.

For catching, killing and eating it had around 48 teeth in total, 26 slim, pointed teeth in its upper jaw and 22 in the lower one.

Using warm thermals to take off and soar through the air, Tropeognathus would travel many miles in search of food. It tended to remain near water, resting on cliffs as it went but rarely venturing very far inland where it might get hunted.

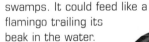

Dinosaur Data

PRONUNCIATION:	TROP-EE-OG-NAY-THUSS
SUBORDER:	PTERASAURIA
DESCRIPTION:	SCAVENGING BIRD
DIET:	FISH AND SQUID

NEW DINOSAUR DISCOVERIES

New dinosaur fossils are being discovered all the time. Here are a few of the most interesting new dinosaurs discovered and named during recent years.

Dilong paradoxus ("paradoxical emperor dragon")

Found: Liaoning Province, China, in 2004
Named: 2004
Period: Lower Cretaceous

This tiny cousin of Tyrannosaurus Rex (see page 54) was covered in primitive hair-like feathers, which probably kept it warm. It was 1.6 m (5 ft) long and weighed around 11 kg (24 lb). Scientists hope that further study of this dinosaur will tell them a lot about the evolution of the tyrannosaurid family. The discovery of a tyrannosaurid with feathers is particularly exciting, because this is the dinosaur family believed to have evolved into birds!

Europasaurus holgeri ("Holger's lizard from Europe")

Found: Northern Germany, in 1998
Named: 2006
Period: Jurassic

This dinosaur was named in June 2006. It belongs to the **sauropod** family. It grew to about the size of a horse, whereas some of its cousins were bigger than buses.

Scientists think it lived on an island. The island could not support larger dinosaurs, so Europasaurus rapidly became smaller, to suit its habitat and food supply.

Microraptor ("little thief")

Found: China, in 1999
Named: 2000
Period: Cretaceous

This **bipedal** carnivore was only about 70 cm (28 in.) long and weighed 1–2 kg (2–4 lb). Its feet were adapted for climbing and it probably lived in trees. It body was thickly covered with feathers, and it had two sets of wings! This may be the most bird-like dinosaur yet found.

Microraptor fossil

Yinlong ("hidden dragon")

Found: Xinjiang Province, China, in 2004
Named: 2006
Period: Late Jurassic

This small herbivore (1.2 m; 4 ft long) is the oldest **ceratopsian** dinosaur ever found, a very early relative of Triceratops (see page 136). It was still small and light enough to walk on its hind legs. Its name comes from the title of the film *Crouching tiger, hidden dragon*, which was filmed close to where its fossils were discovered.

Sauroposeidon
("lizard earthquake God")

Found: Oklahoma, USA in 1994
Named: 1999
Period: Early/Mid Cretaceous

This giant herbivore had longest neck of any dinosaur yet found. It weighed about 60,000 kg (60 tons) and was 18 m (60 ft) tall. It could have raised its head to look in at a six-storey window.

Paralititan

Paralititan ("tidal giant")

Found: Egypt, 2000
Named: 2001
Period: Cretaceous

This giant **herbivore** weighed 50,000 kg (50 tons). It was 27 m (90 ft) long and 9 m (30 ft) tall. Scientists think it may have lived in mangrove swamps.

Mapusaurus roseae
("Earth-lizard from the rose-coloured rocks")

Found: Patagonia, Argentina (South America), in 1997
Named: 2006
Period: Late Cretaceous

At over 12 m (39 ft) long, this huge **carnivore** was bigger than Tyrannosaurus Rex! It weighed over 8,000 kg (8 tons).

It looked much like Tyrannosaurus Rex, but had a longer and narrower skull. Scientists believe it may have hunted in packs that might even have brought down Argentinosaurus (see page 96).

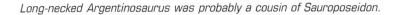

Long-necked Argentinosaurus was probably a cousin of Sauroposeidon.

FOSSIL HUNTING

The only knowledge of dinosaurs comes from fossils. These are often parts of skeletons, but footprints, eggs and occasionally, remains of skin and even droppings have been found.

The discovery of a site can happen by accident, for example, discovering remains while carrying out other work, or alternatively by planned digging with the aim of finding fossils.

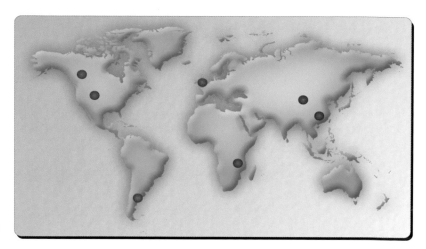

Dinosaurs inhabited all the continents, although at that time the continents were in different places to where they are now. The climates were also quite different. Most fossils are those of sea animals, particularly those that lived in shallow water near the coast, where mud and silt were constantly present to bury their dead remains. As dinosaurs were all land animals, there are very few fossils because their bodies were usually eaten by scavengers or scattered in the wind. If the remains were covered quickly however, a few fossils survived. Sometimes the remains were washed into a nearby stream or river and eventually found their way into a lake or seabed, where they became fossilised.

First fossils

The first dinosaur fossils to be studied scientifically came from western England. The countries where particularly large numbers of dinosaur remains have been found include the United States, Canada, China, Mongolia, Argentina and Tanzania. However, not all of the regions of the world have been investigated fully.

Extraction of fossils

Palaeontologists uncovering a site containing the remains of dinosaurs use techniques that enable them to extract the fossils in the best possible condition. These techniques ensure that we can gather the best possible information about the fossils and prevent any damage during transport to the laboratory to analyse them. There, the fossils are prepared and made available for scientific study and then exhibition to the public.

Having worked out the rough shape of a bone, the surrounding rock needs to be cut away to leave a block. This is then wrapped in a shell of paper and strips of cloth soaked in plaster which, once they have hardened, make it possible to remove the entire block and transport it without breaking or disturbing the fossil inside.

The scientific investigation begins in the field, with a detailed note being made of the position of the bones, in order to record how they are arranged on the site, and the types of rock that surround them.

The remaining surrounding rock is removed using small tools, or dissolved with acid. Once laboratory preparation is complete, each bone is described, measured and analysed in order to identify the animal as precisely as possible and to find out whether it is a new species.

WHY DID DINOSAURS DIE OUT?

The dinosaurs lived for more than 150 million years and were the most successful group of animals ever.

They *all* died out 65 million years ago, as did the flying reptiles and most of the sea reptiles. Seventy percent of all species on earth died. This is called **the K-T Extinction Event**.

Most scientists blame a combination of two things:

- a meteorite hitting the Earth (this is called *the impact theory*)
- massive volcanic eruptions.

Impact theory

When the meteorite hit the Earth it made a huge explosion, destroying everything within an area between 400 km (250 miles) and 500 km (312 miles) across. It threw up massive dust clouds that blocked the sunlight, caused huge forest fires, storms and tidal waves. The impact set off a chain reaction of earthquakes and volcanic eruptions. Weather patterns all over the planet changed.

The fires, storms and tidal waves would have killed large numbers instantly. The fires wiped

Meteorite

out massive areas of plant life. After the strike, the Earth was surrounding by clouds of dust, shutting out sunlight for about six months. It became very cold, dusty and dark, making it hard for animals to live and breathe. Without sunlight, plant life died. **Herbivores** starved and so did **carnivores** that preyed on them.

The meteorite impact shook the Earth. Deep cracks opened up in the landscape, and earthquakes would have made previously safe areas dangerous to live in.

At the same time as the meteor hit Earth, volcanoes all over the planet erupted — they poured out red-hot lava (liquid rock) that burned everything it touched. Much of the land surface where dinosaurs lived got covered in layers of molten rock. The volcanoes also

Plant eater Sauropod

threw dust and poisonous gases into the air. Some of these were breathed in, others fell back to Earth in acid rain.

Underwater volcanoes erupted, sending water from the sea's bed to the surface. This deep-sea water was low in oxygen and killed most of the plankton living at the surface. The marine reptiles died because some of them fed on the plankton, and others fed on the plankton-eaters.

Other theories

Here are a few of the other theories.

- The climate was cooling. Dinosaurs were unable to adapt to the new conditions.

- Falling sea levels reduced the habitat available to marine and shallow-water dwellers.

- As oceans began to dry up, more land bridges appeared. Dinosaurs could walk across these into new areas looking for food. They came into contact with other dinosaurs, and passed on diseases to which they had no immunity.

- The herbivores ate too much of the Earth's vegetation and so ran out of food. Once the herbivores were gone, the carnivores had nothing to eat and died out too.

- Snakes, lizards, birds and other small animals survived. It is not known why some species survived the K-T Extinction and others did not.

Archeoceratops

Erupting volcano

SYNAPSIDS

The sauropsida class includes all reptiles (such as dinosaurs) and, further down the evolutionary scale, all birds as well. The synapsida class contains the pelycosaurs (such as Dimetrodon (see page 16)), the therapsids (ancestors of mammals) and mammals. Mammals are the only surviving synapsids but they are also the dominant land animal on Earth, at least at present, and contained one of the largest known animals – the blue whale.

Pelycosaurs

The very earliest known synapsid is called Archaeothyris. It lived during the Carboniferous period (350 to 300 million years ago) and was one of a group of early synapsids called pelycosaurs that were very successful; they became the dominant land animals in the late Carboniferous and early Permian periods. They were cold-blooded creatures with small brains.

Synapsids are creatures that have a single hole on each side of their skull, where the jaws attach. In the Permian period (300–248 million years ago), there were two types of animals – synapsids, which were the ancient ancestors of mammals, and sauropsids.

Therapsids

The therapsids were an advanced group of synapsids that appeared during the first half of the Permian era and by the middle and late Permian era had become the dominant creatures. This group included both **carnivores** and **herbivores** and ranged in size from tiny rat-sized creatures to bulky herbivores weighing as much as 1,000 kg (2,200 lb).

The great extinction

Therapsids remained dominant for millions of years, until a series of massive volcanic eruptions wiped out over 70% of all land dwelling creatures and 90% of all those that dwelt in the vast seas. This was the single most devastating extinction in the entire history of life to date. Though greatly reduced in numbers, a few therapsids did survive into the new Triassic era. However, none of the pelycosaurs survived.

The surviving therapsids were split into three main groups: beaked herbivores called dicynodonts, many of which had a pair of tusk-like teeth (like Lystrosaurus); the cynodonts (see page 210), and finally the therocephalians, a group that did not last beyond the early Triassic period.

Synapsids vs sauropsids

By the early Triassic period, the synapsids were accompanied by sauropsids such as the early archosaurs, some of which were small and lightly built whilst others were as big as, or bigger than, the largest therapsids. Most of these early sauropsids were carnivores whose reptilian metabolism

was well suited to the arid and strong monsoon climates of the single great landmass of **Pangaea**, giving them a distinct advantage over the therapsids. So whereas in the Permian period the synapsids had dominated, now it was the turn of the sauropsids.

Dimetrodon

CYNODONTS

Cynodont means 'dog teeth' and is the name given to the direct ancestors of the mammals. These creatures lived during the Triassic and early Jurassic periods at the same time as the archosaurs (the ancestors of the dinosaurs).

Teeth and jaws

The cynodonts had teeth that had many points rather than just one. This meant that they could have much more specialised diets. The teeth of the lower and upper jaw met over a broad area when the mouth was closed, so they were able to grind and chew food more efficiently.

As well as having different types of teeth, the jaw of the cynodonts had a reduced number of jaw bones compared to the earlier synapsids. The 'spare' bones became parts of the mammal's inner ear. Improved hearing gave these creatures a better awareness of their environment – a definite advantage – this also meant that they needed to be able to process more information in their brains, leading to larger brains.

Evolution

Cynodonts also developed a secondary palate in the roof of the mouth. This allowed air to flow to the lungs through the back of the mouth, allowing cynodonts to chew and breathe at the same time. This characteristic is present in all mammals today except adult humans.

Unlike the dicynodonts, which remained large, the cynodonts became progressively smaller and more mammal-like as time went on. The largest cynodonts were roughly the size of a wolf and were much smaller than the archosaurs that were around at the same time.

Whether through changing climate, changing vegetation, competition from other creatures, or a combination of factors, most of the large cynodonts and dicynodonts had disappeared before the Jurassic era. Their places were taken by the archosaur's descendants – the dinosaurs. The cynodonts that survived were smaller and evolved into the earliest mammals.

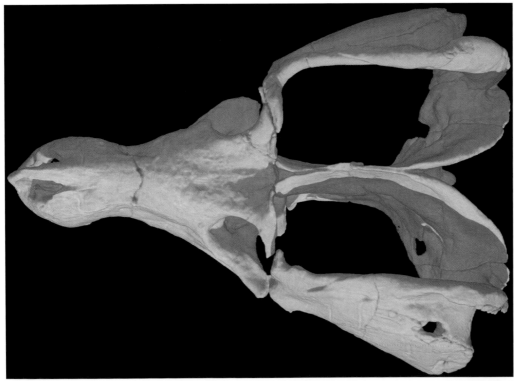

Cynodont skull

Cynognathus (sy-nog-NAY-thus)

This wolf-sized cynodont lived in the mid-Triassic period, about 245–230 million years ago. It was a swift carnivorous quadruped with powerful jaws sporting a wide variety of teeth — sharp incisors, long canines and shearing cheek teeth. It was a pack hunter, its principal prey being herbivorous therapsids such as Kannemeyeria.

Cynognathus was roughly 1.5 m (5 ft) long, was probably warm-blooded and may have been hairy — although we cannot know this for certain as soft-tissues 'like hair' do not survive fossilisation.

It's name means 'dog jaw' and was given by H.G. Seeley in 1876. Fossils have been found in Argentina and South Africa.

Fossilised head of Cynognathus crateronotus

EARLY MAMMALS

The earliest mammals evolved in the Triassic period alongside the archosaurs, after the great extinction that marked the end of the Permian period.

Mammals evolved from the cynodonts (see page 210). Like other synapsids they have only one hole in their skull where the jaw muscles attach. However, unlike other synapsids they have mammary glands – organs that in the females of the species produce milk for the young. This feature is unique to mammals.

Mammals possess another unique feature, a section of the brain called the neo-cortex. This is associated with the senses, movement and awareness of space and, in humans, language and thought.

The very first mammal is widely accepted to have been Megazostrodon, a sleek, tiny **quadruped** with a long tail and long snout. This little creature probably ate insects, measured about 10 cm (4 in.) long and weighed about 200 g (8 oz). A complete fossilised skeleton was found in Lesotho (in South Africa).

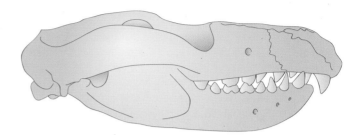

Most of the early mammals were small, shrew-like nocturnal scurrying creatures that lived primarily by hunting insects. In 2000 fossils of a mammal named Repenomamus measuring approximately 1 m (3 ft) long were found in China.

A mammal fossil was found in China, with the fossilised remains of a small dinosaur in its stomach (a young Psitticasosaurus (see page 152)), indicating that larger mammals preyed on dinosaurs! This dramatically altered the view of how early mammals coexisted with the dinosaurs.

However, even the larger specimens of mammals were in the shadow of the dinosaurs until the dinosaurs became extinct.

Megalostrodon fossil

Monotremes

Whilst they survived the cataclysmic impact that ended the age of the dinosaurs, the multituberculata became extinct about 34 million years ago (roughly 30 million years after the dinosaurs).

Monotremes ('single opening') have several features that distinguish them from other mammals. Firstly their reproductive, urinary and anal tracts all open into a single duct (called the cloaca), this feature is the one that gave rise to their name; secondly they lay eggs rather than give birth to live young and, whilst they have mammary glands, they have no nipples – milk for the newly hatched young is instead secreted from the skin along their underbellies.

There were once many kinds of monotremes but only two survive – the duck-billed platypus and the spiny anteater (also known as Echidna). Both these families are now only native to Australia and New Guinea, although in 1991 a fossilised tooth from a monotreme was found in Argentina.

Multituberculata

This mammal subclass first appeared during the middle of the Jurassic period. They were small and rodentlike. They were distinguished by their teeth, which had multiple points arranged in rows, these points are also sometimes referred to as "tubercles", hence multituberculata or "many points."

The bat is the only mammal that can truly fly, rather than simply glide.

MARSUPIALS

There are around 330 species of marsupials today. Probably the best-known marsupial is the kangaroo.

The earliest fossil of a marsupial yet discovered was found in China in 2003 and belongs to a species called Sinodelphys szalayi. This little creature was about the size of a chipmunk, being 15 cm (6 in.) long from nose to tail and weighed only about 30 g (1 oz). It probably spent most of its time scampering through the branches of trees as it hunted worms, grubs and other insects. This ability to climb would also have helped it evade predators.

The largest marsupial ever to have existed is Diprotodon, at 1.7 m (5 ft) tall, and weighing up to 2,500 kg (5,000 lb). It was a **quadruped** and an **herbivore**. The strong claws on its front may have allowed it to dig up roots to supplement its grazing. Several fossilised footprints have been found. These still bear the impressions of fur so we know that Diprotodon was definitely a furry giant!

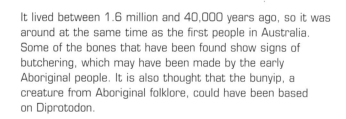

It lived between 1.6 million and 40,000 years ago, so it was around at the same time as the first people in Australia. Some of the bones that have been found show signs of butchering, which may have been made by the early Aboriginal people. It is also thought that the bunyip, a creature from Aboriginal folklore, could have been based on Diprotodon.

Thylacoleo Carnifex

Thylacoleo Carnifex, the 'marsupial lion' lived from about 24 million years ago right up until 50,000 years ago (the end of the last Ice Age). It was a quadruped, about 1.5 m (5 ft) long and may have weighed over 200 kg (440 lb). It had very strong forelimbs and retractable claws. Scientists believe it could climb trees, perhaps dragging prey up there to eat in safety.

The marsupial lion's teeth and jaw were really special. It had very large incisors (sharp teeth for tearing into meat) and calculations show that it would have had the strongest bite of any mammal species, extinct or living. A 100 kg (220 lb) marsupial lion's bite would have been stronger than that of a 250 kg (550 lb) African lion.

This impressive beast is very similar to a mythical creature called the dropbear from Australian Aboriginal folklore – this creature used to lurk in trees and drop upon unwary travellers!

Thylacinus

The last marsupial carnivore to have existed is Thylacinus, also known as the marsupial wolf or Tasmanian tiger. This animal was about the size of a tiger and a cunning predator, though unlike the wolf it hunted alone. It could open its jaws further than any other mammal!

Sinodelphys szalayi fossil

Dinosaur tracks

Thylacinus was common in Tasmania in the 19th century, but its numbers were greatly reduced in the late 19th and early 20th century and it is now thought to be extinct. The last known Thylacinus died in captivity in 1936. However, scientists have recently been investigating the possibility of cloning a Thylacinus from preserved samples.

PLACENTALS

Placentals are now the dominant subclass of mammals. There are almost 4,000 different species of them – including mice, cats, dogs, whales, dolphins and humans. The name placentals refers to the placenta, an organ in the female that forms the connection between the mother and the foetus and helps to nourish the foetus and filter waste.

Eomaia scansoria

The first placental mammal is widely believed to be Eomaia scansoria ('climbing dawn mother'). Its fossil was found in Yixin in China in 2000 and is approximately 125 million years old, indicating that it lived in the early Cretaceous period when the dinosaurs dominated the planet.

Like the majority of early mammals, it was a small rodent-like creature, about 10 cm (4 in.) long and weighing 20–25 g (1 oz). Tiny details are visible, including the tiny bones of its feet and even its fur!

Some scientists have recently disputed whether Eomaia was a true placental mammal, suggesting it may instead have been one of the immediate ancestors of this line instead.

Whales

The largest placental mammal ever to have existed is the blue whale. The largest recorded specimen was 33.5 m (109 ft) long and weighed 190,000 kg (190 tons)! The blue whale is also the loudest creature recorded – its call could be heard underwater for hundreds of miles and reach up to 188 decibels, which is louder than a jet engine! Whales are the only mammals that have evolved to live in the open ocean and one of only two mammals that spend their entire lives in water (the other is the manatee or sea cow).

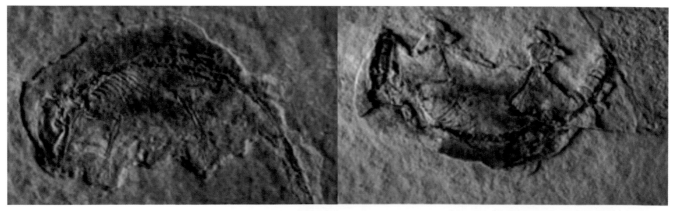

Two fossils of Eomaia scansoria

Dolphin

Fossil records show that whales evolved from hoofed mammals, who adapted to return to the ocean. The oldest whale fossil known, of *Himalayecetus subathuensis*, is 53.5 million years old and was found in the foothills of the Himalayan mountain range in India (an area which was underwater at that time!). This primitive whale was about 3 m (10 ft) long and had functional legs, indicating it may have spent some of its time on land.

Andrewsarchus

The largest land-based carnivorous placental mammal is thought to have been Andrewsarchus. This heavily built wolf-like predator roamed the world from 60 million years ago to roughly 32 million years ago. It was about 4–5m (13–16 ft) long and weighed up to 2,000 kg (2 tons)! Its huge 1 m (3ft) skull contained large sharp teeth for tearing meat, and flatter cheek teeth that may have

been used for crushing bones. Unlike the wolf which it is thought to have resembled, Andrewsarchus had hoofed feet. It is believed it may have been an ancestor of the whales. The first fossil of this creature was found in Mongolia in 1923 by Kan Chen Pao and was named after Roy Chapman Andrews, the palaeontologist who led the expedition.

EARLY CARNIVORES

The order of mammals called the 'carnivora' evolved about 55 million years ago (roughly 10 million years after the extinction of the dinosaurs) and eventually gave rise to the canine and feline predators like wolves and lions.

Carnivora have enlarged canine teeth (the sharp single-pointed teeth at the front of the jaw, near the middle) and one pair of the molars (the teeth at the back of the jaw) are sharp and bladelike, coming together in a scissor like action when the jaw shuts. Both types of teeth are adaptations that are very useful for tearing and slicing meat.

Creodonts

Initially, the dominant carnivores were a group of mammals called the Creodonts. Creodonts remained the dominant carnivores until about 30 million years ago, when they began to decline. One possible reason for this is competition with the carnivora, who had larger brains and a more efficient method of running.

Carnivora

The earliest carnivora belonged to a group called *Miacids*, small creatures rather like modern pine-martens, with long bodies, short legs and long tails. Their paws were wide with the toes spread quite far apart and the first digit opposed to the others (like a human thumb is opposed to the fingers). They would have been good climbers, especially with their long tails to use for balance. These early carnivores primarily ate lizards, birds and smaller shrew-like mammals as well as invertebrates.

Mongoose

Caniforms and feliforms

These earliest carnivores evolved into two distinct families, the caniforms and the feliforms. The caniforms were dog-like carnivores that gave rise to dogs, bears, raccoons and martens. The feliforms were the cat-like carnivores and gave rise to cats, hyenas and mongeese.

Sabre-tooths

Perhaps the most famous of the prehistoric carnivores is the sabre-toothed cat. These creatures were powerful feliform carnivores with long wickedly sharp canine teeth, which could be well over 10 cm (4 in.) long!

Probably the best known sabre-tooth is Smilodon. This awe-inspiring predator evolved around 2 million years ago and survived until about 10,000 years ago. It was about 1.5 m (5 ft) long, 1 m (3 ft) tall and weighed over 200 kg (440 lb), with canine teeth 18 cm (7 in.) long! It was adept at springing onto prey but was a fairly slow runner. This has lead some scientists to speculate that it hunted in packs – some members of the pack would startle prey and drive them out so other members could catch and kill them. Other evidence to support this idea comes from fossils of Smilodons

that had recovered from quite severe wounds. As they would have been unable to hunt their own prey whilst they were healing, some scientists have suggested that they instead fed on the leftovers from kills made by the other members of the pack.

There were many species of sabre-tooths, not all of whom were cats. One example is Thylacosmilus, which lived 3 million years ago. It had huge canine teeth but it was a marsupial and so more closely related to the kangaroo than the cat family.

Skeleton of Smilodon

FICTIONAL DINOSAURS

Dinosaurs in books

A popular theme in stories featuring dinosaurs is the discovery of a 'lost world' where dinosaurs still roam.

Journey to the Centre of the Earth is a science-fiction story written by Jules Verne, and published in 1864. It tells the story of an eccentric professor who leads his nephew and a hired guide to the 'centre of the Earth'. Here they find a whole world of danger, including many prehistoric animals – they are almost eaten by an ichthyosaur, which they observe fighting and killing a plesiosaur.

The Lost World was written by Sir Arthur Conan-Doyle and published in 1912. The eccentric Professor Challenger leads a party of adventurers on an expedition to a mysterious plateau in the Amazon, where dinosaurs still survive. Among the dinosaurs they discover are pterodactyls, one of which they capture and take back to England. There it escapes, leaving the adventurers unable to prove their story!

Michael Crichton's novel *Jurassic Park* and its sequel *The Lost World* featured dinosaurs that had been created by scientists from fossilised genetic material of the extinct creatures, and put into an island theme park.

Dinosaurs are a popular choice for children's books. In the 'Harry and His Bucketful of Dinosaurs' series, Harry jumps into his bucket of toy dinosaurs and is magically transported to 'Dino World', where his toys are now full-sized living dinosaurs.

Dinosaurs on the big screen

Gertie the Dinosaur made her debut in 1914. A cartoonist called Winsor McCay makes a bet with some of his artist friends that he can bring a dinosaur to life. He draws Gertie, and when she comes to life Winsor steps into the cartoon and joins her. A model of Gertie can be seen beside a lake at Disneyland in Florida.

The Lost World was first turned into a film in 1925. This film has been remade four times.

The characters in *King Kong*, a film made in 1933, encountered a fierce Stegosaurus and a meat-eating Apatosaurus. In reality both these dinosaurs were plant-eaters! Kong also battles a Tyrannosaurus Rex, defeating it and going on to fight both a pterosaur and a plesiosaur.

Various dinosaurs featured in the animated Walt Disney film *Fantasia* in 1940; the dinosaurs appeared in the musical sequence *The Rite of Spring*.

Dinosaur was a feature film released in 2000. It was made by Walt Disney Pictures, combining real backgrounds with computer-animated dinosaurs. It follows the adventures of a young Iguanodon, Aladar, as he travels with a herd of peaceful dinosaurs toward their traditional nesting ground. Aladar and some of the weaker dinosaurs – a Brachiosaurus, a Styracosaurus and an Ankylosaurus – are left behind by the herd, but save the day when the herd is attacked by the vicious predator Carnotaurus.

Jurassic Park and its sequels brought dinosaurs to the big screen in realistic detail. The films use the recreation of extinct dinosaurs to give us an exciting adventure story, and also to warn about the dangers that greed and the irresponsible use of science can create.

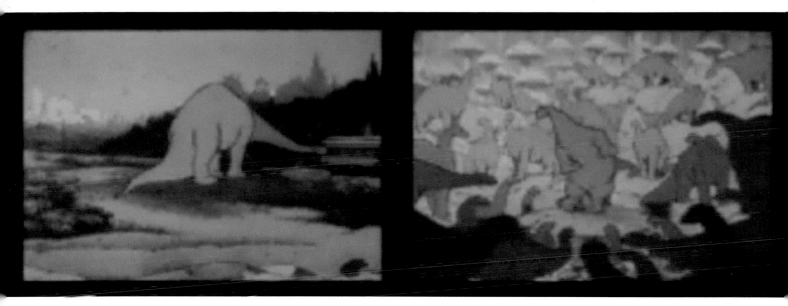

A famous screen dinosaur is Rex, the green toy dinosaur from the films *Toy Story 1* and *2* – a shy dinosaur who was always afraid that he wasn't being 'scary enough'.

Cartoon dinosaurs

Dino appeared in *The Flintstones*, an American cartoon series that became one of the most successful TV cartoon series ever. Dino was the dinosaur pet of the Flintstones, a prehistoric family of cavemen. He behaved much like a pet dog. The Flintstones – and Dino – have appeared in two movies, *The Flintstones* (1994) and *The Flintstones in Viva Rock Vegas* (2000).

The animated film *The Land Before Time* and its eleven sequels feature the adventures of an orphaned Apatosaurus called Littlefoot. His friends are other young dinosaurs:

- *Cera*, a tough and bossy female Triceratops

- *Ducky*, a sweet, loyal female Saurolophus

- *Petrie*, a Pterodactyl who is afraid of flying

- *Spike*, an ever-hungry Stegosaurus.

The gang of friends have many adventures, and learn much about life, all the while avoiding the dreaded 'sharpteeth' (carnivores).

FICTIONAL DINOSAURS

Dinosaurs on television

In the early 1990s, dinosaurs even got their own soap opera! *Dinosaurs* was a live-action comedy with humans inside dinosaur costumes, their voices provided by actors. The show featured a family of 'civilised dinosaurs', the Sinclairs, who faced many of the same issues as people. All the members of the family were different dinosaurs – the father, Earl, was a Megalosaurus, while his wife, Fran, appeared to be an Allosaurus.

In 1974, the science-fiction series *Doctor Who* had a story *Invasion of the dinosaurs* in which prehistoric dinosaurs were brought to London by a time machine.

Dinosaurs in computer games

Dinosaurs feature in video games. Here are just some of them.

- **Prince Tricky** in the *Star Fox* universe. Tricky is a Triceratops.

- In the **Dino Crisis** series, players battled dinosaurs from the past.

- In **Dino Stalker,** the hero was a World War II pilot who was shot down and regained consciousness in prehistoric times.

- **Greymon** and **MetalGreymon** are characters in the monster game and cartoon series *Digimon*.

Dinosaur 'celebrities'

Here are two dinosaur 'celebrities'.

Barney
Barney and friends is a TV show. Barney, a purple dinosaur who looks vaguely like a tyrannosaur, helps young children to

learn through songs and games. Barney was created in 1987, and *Barney and friends* was first shown in 1992.

Godzilla
Godzilla was a radioactive prehistoric monster who attacked Tokyo and other Japanese cities in a series of films. Godzilla was subjected to nuclear radiation and, as a result, grew to giant size and gained unusual powers. Godzilla has appeared in more than 28 Japanese films. Godzilla also appeared in less villainous form in his own cartoon series, gaining the younger and smaller companion Godzuki. In 1998, a new film was made by TriStar Pictures, set in modern day New York.

DRAGONS

were said to wrap their victims in their coils and crushed them to death – just like a large constrictor snake.

Over time, these – and possibly other – elements all came together to give us what we think of as dragons – fearsome lizard-like monsters with wings, who could breathe fire. They were thought to guard great hoards of treasure and are often used in stories to symbolise greed.

The closest thing to a living dragon now is the komodo dragon from the East Indies. This is a great monitor lizard and is the largest living lizard in the world, 2–3 m (6–9 ft) long, equipped with sharp teeth and long, powerful claws. Komodo dragons are effective hunters – they have even on rare occasions been known to kill people.

Many people think that the discovery of huge fossilised bones from creatures that must have looked like huge lizards helped to create the myth of dragons.

In the West, dragons have always been considered evil and monstrous, whereas in the East, especially in China, they are revered as wise and powerful.

Dragons do have other traits that are hard to explain just by the discovery of dinosaur bones. For example, it is almost compulsory for Western dragons to breathe fire. It may be that the sight of fiery meteorites and comets in the ancient night sky gave birth to the idea of flying, fire-breathing monsters – comets were often referred to in medieval times as 'dragon stars'.

Most of the earliest dragons are described as legless. The word dragon comes from the Latin word *draco* (snake). These giant monsters

Viking boat prow showing dragon head

224

DRAGON DATA

- The red dragon is the national symbol of Wales. Probably the most famous dragon in Britain, it is called Y Draig Goch in Welsh. Dragons appear in many tales of Celtic mythology. In the *Mabinogion* a red dragon fights a white dragon which is trying to invade Britain. The fighting dragons create a terrifying noise and King Lludd lures them to fall into a pit full of mead. They drink the alcoholic mead and fall asleep. Legend has it they are still there, imprisoned under Snowdonia, the highest mountain in Wales.

- A dragon named Tiamat features in the Babylonian creation myth – she was slain by the greatest hero of the gods, Marduk, who split her body in two and used half of it to create the Earth and the other half to create the sky.

- St George, the patron saint of England, is famous for slaying a dragon. This did not take place in England, however, but in far-off Syria!

- Dragons feature in the oldest known epic tale – the *Epic of Gilgamesh* from around 3000 BC.

- Raiding Vikings carved fierce dragon heads on the prows of their longboats to strike terror into the hearts of their enemies.

- The constellation of *Draco* – the Dragon – is found between the Great Bear (the Plough) and the Little Bear.

- In medieval times, dishonest people wishing to make money from displaying 'marvels' faked the remains of 'baby dragons' using lizard bodies and the wings of bats.

- The 17th century English term *dragoon* for soldiers that had horses but dismounted to fight on foot, came from the 'fire-spitting' wide-bore muskets that they used. (A musket is a very primitive form of gun.)

CHINESE DRAGONS

The oldest dragon stories come from China. Eastern dragons have usually been considered benevolent (kind). They look different too – they do not usually have wings, and have a snake-like body, several clawed feet like those of an eagle, feathery manes and huge eyes. They are often shown holding a magic pearl that allows them to control lightning. They also have horns like a stag.

Chinese dragons were believed to have control over the elements, and so the weather. They brought the vital rains, and commanded all areas of water – lakes, seas, rivers and oceans. They are associated with wisdom, and long life.

Eastern dragons probably originated as tribal animal totems, which depicted animals in a highly stylised way, and often combined the attributes and body parts of various creatures.

Dragons evolved from this to be seen as mythical creatures. They were said to have the power to change shape.

Dragons were strongly associated with water and there were thought to be four major Dragon Kings who represented the Seas of the East, West, North and South.

Dragons were portrayed in art and decoration in different ways, using a kind of code: a dragon embroidered onto silk with five claws meant a king; four claws were for a prince; and just three meant a lesser courtier.

The dragon was a symbol of imperial authority for many Chinese dynasties. The legendary First Emperor, the Huang Di (the Yellow Emperor) used the symbol, and was said to have turned into a dragon when he died and ascended to heaven. The imperial throne was named the Dragon Throne. Because he was the first Emperor, there is an old folk custom of the Chinese people referring to themselves as 'children of the dragon'.

DRAGON DATA

- The Mandarin Chinese word for dragon is 'leong'.

- One of the 12 signs of the Chinese Zodiac is the Dragon. People born in the years of the Dragon are said to be honest, brave, healthy, energetic and generous.

- There is a Chinese proverb that runs 'hoping one's child will become a dragon' – this means, they hope the child will grow up to be as powerful and successful as a dragon.

- In Chinese myth, dragons are associated with good luck.

Today, dragons feature heavily in Chinese celebrations all over the world. At special festivals, such as Chinese New Year, 'dragon boat races' are held. These boats have magnificent carved dragons at the prow, and are rowed by up to 12 people. 'Dragon dancing' can also be seen on festive occasions – large wood-and-cloth dragons, with masks for heads and long bodies, are given life by people who support the dragon with poles and dance it through the streets. These 'dragon dancers' need to be very fit and well-trained.

THE LOCH NESS MONSTER

Loch Ness, in the highlands of Scotland, is a huge lake to have to search – it is 36.8 km (22.8 miles) long and nearly 1.5 km (1 mile) wide. It is also an impressive 137 m (450 ft) deep, plunging to almost 305 m (1,000 ft) in places.

Some people believe that there is a monster in the murky waters of Loch Ness. There have been many reported sightings, but there is still no evidence that the creature exists. Even attempts to find it by searching the entire lake with sonar have failed, though they have produced findings of large objects that cannot be identified. Attempts to find the 'monster' are still being made.

The Life of Saint Columba from the 6th century tells a story of the saint rescuing an unfortunate local from a monster in the River Ness and ordering it into the depths of the lake.

Descriptions

The first alleged modern sighting of the creature was in 1933, and it was then that newspapers first coined the

phrase 'Loch Ness Monster'. Since then people have claimed to see the 'monster' on more than 1,000 occasions. Most of the descriptions share some or all of the following characteristics:

- a serpent-like neck or body
- a snake-like or a horse-like head
- v-shaped ripples in the water
- gaping mouth
- horns or antennae on top of the head
- dark grey colour (like an elephant)
- many accounts describe an animal 'rolling' or 'plunging' in the water.

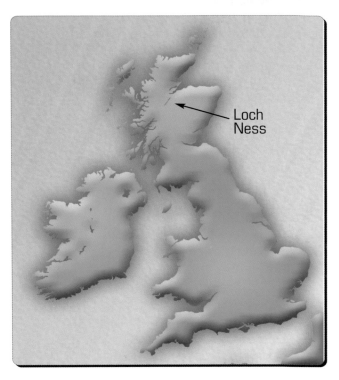

Loch Ness

Theories

Most scientists believe these accounts describe an animal most like an extinct dinosaur – a plesiosaur. Plesiosaurs lived from the late Triassic to the Cretaceous period. The similarity between them and descriptions of the Loch Ness Monster has led some to suggest that a whole breeding colony of plesiosaurs has survived, possibly hidden in caverns beneath the lake. Such a huge underwater cavern was discovered by coastguard George Edwards in 1989.

228

Many biologists say that Loch Ness could not support even a tiny group of such creatures, even if the idea of them surviving for such a length of time were likely.

Other people suggest that a breeding colony of plesiosaurs has survived out in the ocean – and that sometimes babies swim into the loch and grow too big to get out.

Evidence

In 2003, fossil plesiosaur bones were actually found in Loch Ness. However, the scientists who examined them found that the four vertebrae had been brought from elsewhere and planted deliberately.

Most surface photographs of the monster are unclear, and the most famous picture, the 'surgeon's photograph' from the 1930s, has been admitted to be a fake.

In the 1970s, a research group obtained some underwater photographs after scouring the loch with sonar. These pictures seem to show a roughly plesiosaur-shaped creature, in particular close ups of a diamond-shaped 'fin'. People still do not agree whether they show a moving fin or simply bubble patterns in the water.

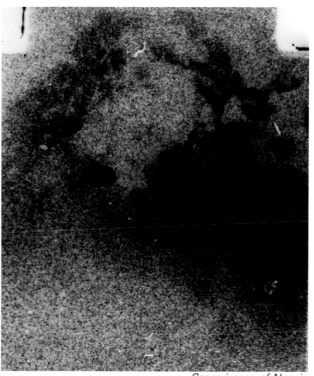

Sonar image of Nessie

PRONUNCIATION GUIDE

A

Acrocanthosaurus	ak-row-KAN-tho-SAWR-us
Allosaurus	AL-uh-SAWR-us
Altirhinus	All-tee-ryne-us
Ankylosaurus	ANG-ki-lo-SAWR-us
Apatosaurus	a-PAT-oh-SAWR-us
Arrhinoceratops	Ay-rye-no-serra-tops
Archaeopteryx	ark-eeOP-ter-iks
Argentinosaurus	ahy-gen-TEEN-oh-SAWR-us

B

Baronyx	BAR-ee-ON-iks
Brachiosaurus	brack-ee-oh-SAWR-us

C

Camarasurus	kuh-MARE-uh-SAWR-us
Camptosaurus	kamp-toe-SAWR-us
Carcharodontosaurus	Kar-kar-owe-don-toe-SAWR-us
Carnotaurus	KAR-no-TAWR-us
Caudipteryx	caw-DIP-ter-iks
Centrosaurus	SEN-tro-SAWR-us
Coelophysis	see-law-FYS-iss
Coelurus	seel-yur-us

Compsognathus	komp-so-NATH-us
Corythosaurus	cor-IH-thoh-SAWR-us

D

Deinonychus	dyn-ON-ik-us
Dimetrodon	die-MET-roe-don
Dimorphodon	die-MORF-oh-don
Diplodocus	dip-LOD-oh-kus
Drinker	DRINK-er
Dromaeosaurus	DROH-mee-oh-SAWR-us
Dryosaurus	dry-owe-SAWR-us

E

Edaphosaurus	ah-DAF-oh-SAW-us
Edmontonia	ed-mon-TONE-ee-ah
Edmontosaurus	ed-MON-toe-SAWR-us
Elasmosaurus	ee-LAZ-moh-sawr-us
Eoraptor	EE-oh-RAP-tor
Eryops	AR-ee-ops

G

Gallimimus	GALL-ih-MIME-us
Gerrothorax	geh-roh-THOR-ax
Gigantosaurus	Jig-a-NOT-oh-SAWR-us
Gryposaurus	grip-owe-SAWr-us

H

Hadrosaurus	HAD-row-SAWR-us
Herrerasaurus	he-ray-raar-SAWR-us
Hesperornis	HES-per-OR-nis
Huayangosaurus	hoo-ah-yang-oh-SAWR-us
Hypacrosaurus	high-pah-kroe-SAWR-us
Hypsilophodon	hip-sill-owe-foe-don

I

Ichthyosaurus	IK-thee-oh-SAWR-us
Iguanodon	ig-WAN-oh-DON

K

Kentrosaurus	KEN-troh-SAWR-us
Kronosaurus	crow-no-sawr-us

L

Leaellynasaura	lee-ell-lin-ah-SAWR-ah

| Leptoceratops | lep-toe-SERR-a-tops |
| Liopleurodon | LIE-oh-PLOO-ro-don |

M

Maiasaura	MY-ah-SAWR-ah
Megalosaurus	MEG-uh-low-SAWR-us
Melanosaurus	mel-uh-NOR-uh-SAWR-us
Microceratops	my-kro-SAYR-ah-tops
Minmi	MIN-mee
Mosasaurus	MOES-ah-SAWR-us

N

| Nodosaurus | noh-doh-SAWR-us |
| Nothosaurus | no-tho-SAWR-us |

O

Opthamosaurus	off-THAL-moh-SAW-rus
Orodromeus	orrow-drom-ee-us
Othnielia	oth-nigh-ell-ee-ah
Oviraptor	o-vih-RAP-tor

P

Panoplosaurus	pan-oh-ploh-SAWR-us
Parasaurolophus	par-ah-SAWR-oh-LOW-fuss
Piatnizkysaurus	Pee-at-nits-key-SAWR-us
Plesiosaurus	PLEE-see-o-SAWR-us
Procomsognathus	pro-comp-son-ay-thus
Protoceratops	pro-toe-SERR-a-tops
Psittacosaurus	SIT-ah-koe-SAWR-us
Pteranodon	ter-an-owe-don
Pterosaur	ter-oh-SAW

Q

| Quetzalcoatlus | kett-zal-coe-at-lus |

R

| Rhamphorhynchus | RAM-for-INK-us |

S

Saltasaurus	salt-ah-SAWR-us
Saltopus	sall-toe-pus
Saurornithoides	SAWR-or-nih-THOY-deez
Scelidosaurus	skel-ee-doh-SAWR-us
Scutellosaurus	sku-TEL-oh-SAWR-us

Seismosaurus	size-moh-SAWR-us
Shonisaurus	SHON-e-SAWR-us
Spinosaurus	SPINE-o-SAWR-us
Stegosaurus	STEG-oh-SAWR-us
Stygimoloch	STIG-ih-MOE-lock
Styracosaurus	sty-rack-oh-SAWR-us

T

Tenontosaurus	ten-on-toe-SAWR-us
Thescelosaurus	thess-kell-owe-SAWR-us
Titanosaurus	tie-TAN-oh-SAWR-us
Triceratops	try-SER-a tops
Troodon	TRUE-oh-don
Tropeognathus	trop-ee-og-nay-thus
Tylosaurus	TIE-low-SAWR-us
Tyrannosaurus	TIE-ran-owe-SAWR-us

U

| Ultrasaurus | ULL-tra-SAWR-us |

V

| Velociraptor | vuh-LOSS-ih-RAP-tor |

GLOSSARY

ammonite extinct marine molluscs, had coiled shells

ancestor animal from which a later, related animal has evolved

ankylosaurs a group of armoured herbivores that lived 76–68 million years ago. There were three main groups of ankylosaurs – ankylosaurids (like Ankylosaurus, see p118–119), polacanthids and nodosaurids 'node lizard' (nodosaurids differed from the other two types of ankylosaur that they had spines sticking outward from their shoulders and neck)

aquatic water-dwelling

archosaurs triassic reptiles, immediate ancestors of the dinosaurs

binocular vision ability to focus on the same thing with two eyes

biped animal that walks on two hind legs

bipedal walks on two legs

bonebed site where many fossils from the same time period have been found

browsing feeding on high-up leaves, trees and shrubs

camouflage colouring allowing an animal to blend in with its surroundings

canine teeth pointed cone-shaped teeth

carnivore a meat eater

carrion dead body (eaten by scavengers)

ceratopsian plant-eating dinosaurs with horned faces

coelurosaurs 'hollow-tail lizards' – early members of this group were very small, but its members in the end included the most likely ancestors of modern birds

cold-blooded cold-blooded creatures rely on their environment to regulate their body temperature

conifer evergreen trees and shrubs

cretaceous last period of the Mesozoic era, 135–65 million years ago

cycad plant like a palm tree with a middle trunk and leaves

descendent animal whose evolution can be traced back to a particular animal or group

dinosaurs land-dwelling reptiles from the Mesozoic era

erosion the wearing away of the Earth's surface by natural forces

evolution process by which one species changes into another, usually over a long period of time

extinction the dying out of an entire species

extinction-level event catastrophe resulting in the extinction of many species at once (mass extinction)

femur main thigh bone

fenestrae gap or holes in bone, from the Latin for windows

fern leafy plant growing in damp places

fibula calf bone

fossil remains preserved in rock

geologist person who studies rock

gingko primitive seed-bearing tree with fan shaped leaves, common in Mesozoic era

grazing feeding on low-growing plants

hadrosaurs duck-billed plant-eating dinosaurs

herbivore an animal which just eats plants

horsetail primitive spore-bearing plant, common in Mesozoic era

ichthyosaurs sea-dwelling prehistoric reptiles

incisor tooth adapted for cutting and gnawing, usually at the front of the mouth

incubate maintain eggs at good temperature for growth and development

invertebrate animal which has no backbone

jurassic period of the Mesozoic era, 203–135 million years ago

Jurassic Coast area of the coast near Lyme Regis in England, where Mary Anning found many of the fossils that made her famous

juvenile young – not yet an adult

K-T Extinction Event extinction event which occurred at the end of the Cretaceous period resulting in extinction of the dinosaurs and many other species

Lesothaurus Triassic dinosaur

lizard scaly-bodied, air breathing reptile with backbone that evolved from amphibians

mammal hairy warm-blooded animal that nourishes young from mammary glands and evolved during Triassic period

marsupial mammals that give birth to young which then develop in mother's pouch

membrane thin layer of tissue protecting embryo in egg

Mesozoic era age of reptiles, 248–65 million years ago which includes Triassic, Jurassic and Cretaceous periods

molars teeth designed for grinding food

mosasaurs types of marine reptiles

omnivore animal which eats a mixed diet of plants and meat

ornithopods beaked, usually bipedal, plant-eating dinosaurs that flourished from the late Triassic to the late Cretaceous (ornithopod means bird feet)

orthacanthus a primitive shark

ossicles pea-sized bones

palaeontologist person who studies fossils

Pangaea the 'super-continent' formed of all Earth's land masses

paravertebrae extra bony plates added to backbone of dinosaur

plesiosaurs large marine reptiles that lived in Mesozoic era (not dinosaurs)

predator animal which hunts other animals to eat

premolars teeth behind the canines and in front of the molars

primates group of mammals, including monkeys, humans and their ancestors

primitive basic, at an early stage of development

pterandons a group of flying reptiles that were usually toothless and had a short tail

pterodophytes a type of fern (a plant)

pterosaurs flying prehistoric reptiles (not dinosaurs but lived at the same time)

quadruped animal that walks on all fours

rhynchorsaurs herbivorous reptiles from Mezozoic era

sauropods giant, plant-eating dinosaurs with long neck, small head and long tail

scavenger animal that feeds on (dead) meat which it finds, rather than hunts

scutes bony protective plates offering defence against attack

semi-bipedal sometimes walks on hind legs, at other times walks on all fours

species a category of living things, plants or animals, refers to related living things capable of breeding with one another to produce young

stegosaurs a group of herbivorous dinosaurs of the Jurassic and early Cretaceous periods, predominantly living in North America and China.

tendons connect muscle to bone

territory the land or area where an animal lives

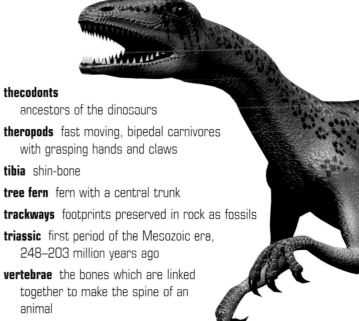

thecodonts ancestors of the dinosaurs

theropods fast moving, bipedal carnivores with grasping hands and claws

tibia shin-bone

tree fern fern with a central trunk

trackways footprints preserved in rock as fossils

triassic first period of the Mesozoic era, 248–203 million years ago

vertebrae the bones which are linked together to make the spine of an animal

vertebrate animal with a backbone

warm-blooded able to keep the body at constant temperature, regardless of the environment

INDEX

INDEX

INDEX

ACKNOWLEDGEMENTS

The authors and publishers would like to thank the following people who played such a significant role in creating this Dinosaur Encyclopedia:

Illustration
HL Studios

Page Design
HL Studios

Editorial
Jennifer Clark, Lucie Williams

Photo Research
Sam Morley

Project Management
HL Studios

Jacket Design
JPX

Production
Elaine Ward

All photographs and other illustrations are copyright of USGS, istockphoto, stockxpert, stockxchnge, Flickr.com, except where stated below:

THE NATURAL HISTORY MUSEUM, LONDON

FOSSILISED DINOSAUR HEART © JIM PAGE / NORTH CAROLINA MUSEUM OF NATURAL SCIENCES / SCIENCE PHOTO LIBRARY

DINOSAUR EXTINCTION © VICTOR HABBICK VISIONS / SCIENCE PHOTO LIBRARY

CONSTRUCTION OF A REPLICA SKELETON OF TITANOSAURUS © PHILIPPE PLAILLY / SCIENCE PHOTO LIBRARY

FOSSILISED HEAD OF CYNOGNATHUS CRATERNOTUS © SINCLAIR STAMMERS / SCIENCE PHOTO LIBRARY

DINOSAUR TRACKS © OMIKRON / SCIENCE PHOTO LIBRARY

SONAR IMAGE OF LOCH NESS MONSTER © MIRRORPIX

BARNEY THE PURPLE DINOSAUR © REUTERS/CORBIS

FLINTSTONES © CAPITAL PICTURES

"HADROSAURUS" BRONZE SCULPTURE BY JOHN GIANNOTTI 2003

A Belani, Belgianchocolate, Bernard Price Institute for Palaeontological Research Adam Morrel, Kaptain Kobold, Kevinzim, Sarah Montani, Lawrence M. Witmer, PhD, Natuurhistorisch Museum Rotterdam (http://www.nmr.nl/), Striatic, Mark Klingler/Carnegie Museum of Natural History, John Sibbick Illustration, Musée d'histoire naturelle de Fribourg, Suisse, Jarbewowski, Maidstone Borough Council, The Academy of Natural Sciences Philadelphia.